By What Authority

Dear Kim + Dave
Be Encouraged.
In Him,
George

By What Authority

Dr. George Edgar Sears

Plumbline Publications
Surrey, B.C.

ENCOURAGING COMMENTS

This book by Dr. Sears is a welcome source of information in our present generation. Given the strength of pluralism today where everyone's voice is of equal authority and value, even though differing from one another, where do we turn for authoritative truth for belief and principles of living? Dr Sears has thoroughly documented the God given inspiration of the Bible. That gives comfort, assurance and authority to all propounding biblical truths. It seems to me that any rational person who realises the Bible is Divine in origin will at the very least give it a listening ear. You need to read this!

Pastor Wes Long

'It is a reference book on different topics that arise in accepting the authority of scripture.' The final chapter, Kindness, is compelling, an expansion of the 'greatest commandment' and 'your neighbor as yourself'. I think this was one of my favourite chapters.

Wendy Hardy

It is a great and timely encouragement to us in this generation, a generation in uncertainty. This is a generation that feels it is hard to find anything they can fully trust, and a generation almost never experiencing a healthy relationship with any authority. *By What Authority* tells people that the Bible is the Book we can trust. I also felt it is about a relationship with God. And, I especially liked the parts where I feel I can hear George's voice :)

Hiroko Yamane

In *By What Authority*, Dr. Sears provides an excellent reminder of the authority and power of Scripture to change the hearts and minds of all men and women who seek Him.

Dr. Colin Godwin, President, Carey Theological College.

By What Authority
Copyright © 2021 George Edgar Sears
All rights reserved.

Plumbline Publications
Surrey, British Columbia

Cover art: Janaye Sears

All rights reserved. No part of this publication may be reproduced, stored in a retrieval system, or transmitted, in any form or by any means, electronic, mechanical, photocopying, recording or otherwise, without the prior written permission of the author, except in the case of brief quotations embodied in crictical articles and reviews.

Scriptures taken from the Holy Bible, New International Version®, NIV®. Copyright © 1973, 1978, 1984, 2011 by Biblica, Inc.™ Used by permission of Zondervan. All rights reserved worldwide. www.zondervan.com The "NIV" and "New International Version" are trademarks registered in the United States Patent and Trademark Office by Biblica, Inc.™

Contents

ENCOURAGING COMMENTS	iv
ACKNOWLEDGEMENTS	ix
PREFACE	xi
INTRODUCTION	xv
The Bible is Like a Plumb Line	xvi
1. BY WHAT AUTHORITY	1
2. A PRICE TO PAY	7
Jeremiah	8
Hosea	23
John, the Baptizer	28
Jesus of Nazareth	31
Bonhoeffer	35
3. CRITIQUE OF THE BIBLE'S AUTHORITY OVER THE CENTURIES	41
John Calvin	42
Roman Catholic Church	45
St. Augustine	46
Spurgeon	50
Biblical Criticism	50
4. A BRIEF HISTORY OF BIBLICAL INSPIRATION	59
5. JESUS' VIEW OF THE SCRIPTURES	73
6. JESUS WAS (is) SUBJECT TO SCRIPTURE	83
Jesus' Death Prophecied	87
7. THE ROLE OF PROPHECY IN SCRIPTURE	93
How Prophecy Ties In The Old And New Testaments	100
8. THE ROLE OF THE HOLY SPIRIT IN SCRIPTURE	111
9. A BELIEVERS' RESPONSE: Kindness	131
Appendix A	143
The Salvation Plan	143
A Simple Prayer for you	147
Appendix B	149
Assurance Of Faith In Christ	149
About the Author	153

BY WHAT AUTHORITY

ACKNOWLEDGEMENTS

This book is dedicated to my wife Judy, who is my constant companion and encourager.

Over the years that I have been considering writing this book, many people have been an influence on me and my ponderings. I am particularly thankful to family: our children and grandchildren, my siblings and of course Judith, my wife of many decades. Special thanks to my granddaughter, Janaye (JMarie), who painted the plumbline cover art.

I also have been influenced by Pastors under whose ministry I have sat during the last ten years or so, over which time this book has been germinating. Each has contributed in some way, as I have reflected on the material in this book, as I have debated in my own mind how I might create and write. Thanks, as well to those who were willing to read this manuscript before it was printed and either did a 'content edit' or wrote a brief endorsement. Thanks to my brother-in-law, Dr. Ken Bellous of Tall Pine Press, who patiently guided me through the challenging process of publication.

Appreciation goes out to Dr. Colin Godwin and the late Dr. Brian Stelck and Dr. Ellis Andre, dear friends with whom I queried and debated the concepts in this book. Thanks as well, to David Wimbish. He is an editor to whom I sent my concept, early in 2020. His response was: "a book of this type is long overdue". Such peer response, as we call it, was an encouragement to me at the time as I prayerfully wrestled with the material.

Further, thanks to those who have listened to me and prayed for me as I have served as a Pastor for nearly four decades. I have written much and learned much as I have produced from one to three sermons a week, over those many decades. Folks have listened and learned. Thanks for being there and being so supportive.

PREFACE

Hi. Browsing? Love to do that too. I have spent much time in book stores, just looking at titles, covers, summaries, subjects and considering the questions that books ask; stories that books tell; information that books provide. Should I get this one or that one? I have left many behind…wondering. Should I go back and get it? Books have contributed much to my life, likely to yours as well. And then in recent decades, articles and podcasts on line. There are so many titles and subjects that continue to interest me.

Also, there are those books that others have insisted I read, as I have moved through several systems of education, many to my benefit of course. And today, someone has referred you to this book or you are looking at this one in a bookstore or on line. What is it about? What a strange title. Well, this book is about a **BOOK**. One that has been around for several thousand years in one form or another. Parts of that book have been around even longer, produced by writers who first *heard,* before they wrote.

Throughout history the Bible has stood the test of critical analysis. It remains today the best-selling written document. Each generation is challenged to consider the Bible as the singular 'Word of God' to the Nations. Throughout the history of Christendom there has been an ongoing debate regarding the implications of the significance that these Scriptures maintain, in the religious discourse. Successive man-made religious written scenarios developed by sincere, devout seekers of 'truth' have occasionally moved into strong positions of significance, for some, through their writings. These written texts have challenged and continue to challenge the veracity of the affirmation that the Bible has a singular importance to all humanity.

This book is being introduced into the discussion to firmly bring the Bible into a position as the only true and faithful Word, given to Humanity. It can play a helpful role for anyone seeking to discover and more fully understand the nature and message of God's Revelation of Himself, to humankind. The book underscores the place of prophecy and the work of the Holy Spirit, over the millennia, in bringing afresh the truth of the Bible's authority to a modern discussion of sacred scriptural text.

Consider that this book you are browsing is written for the average believer who owns a Bible. It researches, illuminates and confirms the significance of the Bible over any other religious writing or oral tradition. What if any, is the difference?

HELLO CHURCH. This book is for YOU. As you may likely know, CHURCH is not a building, a place of meeting, a cathedral or any physical structure where folk meet: it is people all over the world, just like you. This book is intended to be an encouragement to YOU. Some of you have prayed for others, for years, to know Christ. This book is for you. Some of you have used the Bible on a regular basis for your source of inspiration and 'light' for a long time. This book is for you. Some of you have travelled over the world distributing the Bible to strangers, to folk locked in political climates of restriction, totalitarianism or physical imprisonment. This book is for you. Others of you have depended on the Bible as a source for preaching, connecting the truths of Scripture to the variances of culture, over time. You have sensed the Holy Spirit prompting you to think theologically and realistically about life and the meaning of living in your day, amongst your local community, or in communities in specific crisis worldwide. Thank you for your faithfulness. This book is for the 'faithful', meeting with others, worldwide, who trust Jesus as Saviour and Lord.

YOU - BELIEVERS, I trust this work will be an encouragement

for you. What I have written about is not new. Others have studied about the Bible in this way over the centuries but I feel, at this time in history, this message needs to be brought to light again for the sake of the CHURCH in our world. I have been a believer for nearly seven decades. I have seen such change in my country and my world that begs the question as to "what has happened to grace, decency, love of one another, trusted neighbors, kindness and peace on our streets? Why are our communities continuing to be so negative towards others of different race, color, gender, or nationality?" The Bible influences these attitudes, for the better I believe. I write at this time in history because the topic of this book needs to be reconsidered afresh. It has not been addressed for some time. Just as the Church has continued to practice Communion over many centuries because the Bible challenges us to repeat, to 'Remember", so this topic needs to be 'remembered' and then repeated consistently within the Body of Christ. The Church's health is dependent on remembering; we so easily forget, miss a blessing and find ourselves spiritually weak when dealing with life's challenges. So, I write. This topic could change the public discourse in many of the cultures of our present world.

I have not addressed the CHURCH as any denomination. The term *denomination* is always a term with 'history' attached to its understanding. Each Christian denomination has a history, a faithful few or many who have been concerned, as I am, for our world. But those histories, as precious as they are to some of us, are not important in this book. The Church is not a denomination; it is people who trust Jesus Christ as Lord and Saviour; those who have had a personal encounter with Him, at some time of their remembrance. I will refer more to this clarification and Truth, later. (see also Appendix A).

As this book goes to press, our world is in the middle of a pandemic. I trust your reading of this book will end up being a BLESSING to you as you cope with a new normal.

BY WHAT AUTHORITY

INTRODUCTION

I have had the opportunity, over the years, to occasionally build things! As a husband, dad, grandfather and home owner I have been able to get involved with construction for the practical purposes of home ownership. I am privileged in this regard. What father has not spent late hours on Christmas Eve, into Christmas morning, assembling the sought-after gift for their child?

One of the 'tools' I have needed from time to time is what is known as a plumb line. A plumb line is a piece of string with a weight attached to one end, used either to test if something is vertical, such as a wall, is exactly straight, perpendicularity or to find the depth of water. (See Cover). Many years ago, I made my own plumb line, out of necessity. It is simply, as noted, a string with the head of a small discarded hammer, attached. I have used it to determine vertical accuracy in a basement while constructing inner walls of a rec room. I have used it in constructing a shed in our several back yards, in order to have a place to store tools and the like, in fence construction and finally hanging wallpaper. It is this 'tool' which remains in my tool box to this day. The illustration of this tool brings me to an understanding of the significance of the Bible, for this time in our history.

THE BIBLE IS LIKE A PLUMB LINE

The Bible, over the millennia, is understood as a tool for the Hebrew people and for the Church. The Old and New Testaments have a distinct purpose in human history. The Old Testament, amongst other things, indicated to Israel that there was a God, that there was a purpose to their being 'set aside' and blessed amongst all the nations, or tribes as I like to refer to them. It recorded communications between the one true God and His chosen: prophets, leaders, priests and people. The New Testament's purpose, among other things, is to introduce the Church to the world.

The plumb line is a tool. It determines the vertical. The Bible is a tool. It determines a way in which the Creator has decided to communicate with His creation. It measures accurately any other religious writings and sayings over time, from the beginning of time. It measures the truth of those writings. It is the tool which is to be held up against what is being written about the purpose of our lives, the history of the universe, the meaning of life and the conclusion of all of time. A plumb line is a method of measurement based on the simple truth of gravity. Without gravity, there would be no plumb line. And interestingly, the plumb line works anywhere on the earth because its concept is based on gravity, influenced from the center of the earth, pulling the weight downward. In one of several references to a plume line in the Old Testament, Isaiah understood the purpose of this object. "I will make justice the measuring line and righteousness the plumb line" (Isaiah 28:17a). As you shall discover, with me, without the Bible there would be no *truth*, no base line to determine truth.

Consider the following illustration:

In May 2019 Barack Obama spoke to an event at the Canadian Tire Centre called 'Canada 2020'. The context of this comment was the then current dialogue about 'fake news' and its effect on democracies.

He said: "The marketplace of ideas that is the basis of our democratic practice has difficulty working if we don't have some common baseline of what's true and what's not". Democracies have to preserve some 'core social good".[1]

My intention with this book is to give support to this comparison between the use and accuracy of the plumb line to determine the true vertical and the use and accuracy of the Bible considered a baseline, given to us, to everyone, for all time. It is to suggest that no other sacred oral tradition or religious writing, produced in all of human history, is comparable to the Bible. It most accurately enables humankind to discover *Truth*.

By what authority can one claim, as I do, that the Bible is the only written, and initially verbal in many cases, material for an authentic and true understanding of the relationship between the human and the Divine? Between the seen and the unseen? Between the material and the imaginary? The plumb line is an authority based on discovered science, gravity. The Bible is a singular authority based on what? This book will answer that question, which is in the minds of many. A question written about, studied, articulated and PhD'ed (theorized) over many centuries of sincere human investigation.

Finally consider the illustration of our granddaughter, fitting her grade 12 grad dress. The dress is found, purchased and then the granddaughter is brought to the dress for a fitting. The dress needs to fit the girl, not the other way around. It's the same with a religion: the religion needs to be fitted around the Biblical revelation of Jesus, not the other way around.

Endnotes

1. Michelle Zilio, *The Globe and Mail* (theglobeandmail.com, June 1, 2019).

Chapter 1

BY WHAT AUTHORITY

This book title comes from a theme in the Bible, that of *authority*. I wrestled with this concept, so can you. While researching and writing, I recently came across a Memorial service for my wife's grandfather from 1978. In the service while speaking to the family I said: "The Holy Scriptures have been temporarily eroded as society's authority, people can just argue until they convince themselves they are right..." Even back then the germ of this topic has been wrestling in my mind, I suspect.

The need for Jesus to identify His authority to the religious leadership of His day was demanded by them as His ministry unfolded, as understood in the New Testament. By what authority did Jesus speak? According to the Bible, Jesus arrived on the scene doing miracles, healing the sick, raising the dead and challenging evil spirits. As He travelled, His life's work became revealed to the religious leaders of the day, the leaders of the Hebrew faith. This question became important to answer as time went on, as Jesus continued to draw crowds by his ministry. By what authority does He do these things? "Jesus entered the temple courts, and, while he was teaching, the chief priests and the elders of the people came to him. 'By what authority are you doing these things?' they asked. 'And who gave you this authority?'" (Matthew 21:23; see also Mark 11:27-28).

Significant religious leaders who were active at the time of Jesus' life and ministry were the Pharisees and the Sadducees; they understood authority. They viewed themselves as having authority and respect. "The Pharisees and Sadducees came to Jesus and tested him by asking him to show them a sign from heaven" (Matthew 16:1). They were disturbed by His following at the time. John challenged them in his brief ministry. "But when he saw many of the Pharisees and Sadducees coming to where he was baptizing, he said to them: 'You brood of vipers! Who warned you to flee from the coming wrath?'" (Matthew 3:7; Luke 3:7). Jesus repeated the vitriolic challenge to these two groups of religious leaders adding, "You snakes! You brood of vipers! How will you escape being condemned to hell?" (Matthew 23:33, 12:34). Later Jesus continued his condemnation, "Then Jesus said to the crowds and to his disciples: 'The teachers of the law and the Pharisees sit in Moses' seat. So you must be careful to do everything they tell you. But do not do what they do, for they do not practice what they preach'" (Matthew 23:1-3). and, "The Pharisees, who loved money, heard all this and were sneering at Jesus. He said to them, 'You are the ones who justify yourselves in the eyes of others, but God knows your hearts. What people value highly is detestable in God's sight.'" (Luke 16:14-15).

Beyond the record of this attitude noted within the Gospels, the reputation and respect carried by these two groups continued to be of some influence beyond Jesus' resurrection, in the early Church as recorded in Acts 23. Paul the apostle had been brought before the Sanhedrin after having been arrested in Jerusalem because of his growing reputation as a follower of Jesus, who had been crucified. Knowing of the sense of competitive authority owned by these two groups since Paul himself was a Pharisee, he goaded them into a fight which eventually got him freed from the arrest and judgement by these religious leaders, in Jerusalem.

The Israelite prophets of old had a recognized authority. God the Father grants authority. For Jesus to be recognized for His ministry by the religious leaders they needed to come to understand from whence came His authority. Nevertheless, they had difficulty believing in the evidence and eventually did not believe in His authority, given to Him by the Father, through the Holy Spirit. In Matthew and Mark's account of this dialogue, Jesus ended up not giving them the answer to their inquiries.

But the evidence of His authority was there in the work of ministry, in the examples He demonstrated. "When Jesus had finished saying these things, the crowds were amazed at his teaching, because he taught as one who had authority, and not as their teachers of the law" (Matthew 7:28-29).

The people were all so amazed that they asked each other, "What is this? A new teaching—and with authority! He even gives orders to impure spirits and they obey him." (Mark 1:27).

> Very truly I tell you, whoever hears my word and believes him who sent me has eternal life and will not be judged but has crossed over from death to life. Very truly I tell you, a time is coming and has now come when the dead will hear the voice of the Son of God and those who hear will live. For as the Father has life in himself, so he has granted the Son also to have life in himself. And he has given him authority to judge because he is the Son of Man. (John 5:24-27; see also John 2:17ff)

"After Jesus said this, he looked toward heaven and prayed: 'Father, the hour has come. Glorify your Son, that your Son may glorify you. For you granted him authority over all people that he might give eternal life to all those you have given him.'" (John 17:1-2).

And curiously during His ministry, Jesus was able at one point to give His authority over to his disciples as they began their task to proclaim the Kingdom of God which was about to commence, in the succeeding months and years. "When Jesus had called the Twelve together, he gave them power and authority to drive out all demons and to cure diseases, and he sent them out to proclaim the kingdom of God and to heal the sick" (Luke 9:1-2).

Jesus also indicated He had authority to give up his life, which He eventually did. Again in dealing with the Pharisees, Jesus attempted to educate them about His relationship with the Father. In speaking about all people, not just Israel, Jesus used the image of sheep in John 10 and stated, "The reason my Father loves me is that I lay down my life-only to take it up again. No one takes it from me, but I lay it down of my own accord. I have authority to lay it down and authority to take it up again. This command I received from my Father" (John 10:17-18).

After Jesus rose from the dead, according to the scriptures, Matthew 28:18 records, "Then Jesus came to them and said, 'All authority in heaven and on earth has been given to me.'" And finally Peter, one of Jesus' own disciples, later on wrote to the Church and indicated in 1 Peter 3:21b-22, "...It saves you by the resurrection of Jesus Christ, who has gone into heaven and is at God's right hand—with angels, authorities and powers in submission to him." His authority continues until now, for eternity, in the presence of the Father in heaven. The Holy Spirit gave this authority to Jesus.

Authority is a key concept in this book; it must always be questioned. We obey authority over us because we choose to but authority is always given when there is a healthy relationship, with those who have been given authority over us, in any society. SAYS WHO? We all face many forms of the concept and practice of authority. In the Western world and in a healthy democracy, we give authority over to others willingly. In totalitarian societies there is little choice about the authority placed over us. Authority is always either given or taken.

The Bible is different from any other religious writing. It has authority. How so? Demonstrating this fact is the intent of this book. Many religious 'sacred' scriptures exist. Their historical value is important to those of each faith tradition. Such is the case for the Bible and for the Hebrew-Christian belief system. But before looking at the uniqueness of the Bible's authority consider the price some have paid to bring us this Book. Men and women have listened to God the Father over the millennia of time. They have spoken the Words of the

Lord and have written the same, eventually. In some cases, they have used scribes to do the writing. But there were personal costs paid by those who were open to listen to the Father through the influence of the Holy Spirit. How that all came about will be considered in this book but first: there is a personal price to pay to being open to the leading of the Holy Spirit in one's life.

BY WHAT AUTHORITY

Chapter 2

A PRICE TO PAY

There have always been, historically, personal struggles associated with men's or women's lives when they have been 'called of God' to proclaim His words to humankind. God has used and continues to use individuals to declare and maintain the significance of Biblical writings, letters, or prophecies and their influence on people throughout recorded history even including oral tradition. There has always been a challenge for any person, male or female, to be a spokesperson for the Father. The price paid has often been dear.

The Bible has always been considered to have some authority. Does it have the authority that the Church propounds? That it propounds of itself? Is it more authoritative than any other religious writing or verbal oracle? These considerations are central to this book. Proponents making the point of the significance of the Bible have often been challenged, even threatened, jailed or killed, throughout human history. Within the Bible itself, prophets have been threatened because of their dogmatic assertions that the Father has communicated to them and then they to others, who might listen. God has always desired to communicate to Israel as well as the Church and continues to do so. Over time pronouncements were made that God had spoken, by various means, but the words or writings of the prophets have been castigated. They themselves were threatened by those around them, both from within and from outside of the 'faith'. "There is a price to being a prophet".[1]

JEREMIAH

The first prophet to be considered was one of the most significant and memorable prophets to enter the scene as a 'spokesperson for the Father'. His name was Jeremiah. Much of what we know of him comes from the prophecy of Jeremiah in the Old Testament. He demonstrated for us in a very critical and unique way that those who have worked to be spokespersons for the Father, leaving their words and experiences written down eventually to be found within the Bible, were persecuted, beaten, jailed and occasionally killed for their persistence that God was speaking through them, specifically.

We find his story included amongst several other 'major' prophets in the Old Testament like Isaiah, Ezekiel and Daniel. Scholars, over the centuries, have described prophets in the Bible as 'major' or 'minor' based on initially, their messages and influence within Judaism. Further, as we shall consider later, their writings had profound influence on the Israelites over the centuries. And in recent centuries, their prophetic writings have been seen to have had profound influence on anyone seeking to come to an understanding of the Father, His purposes for humankind and for our eternal futures.

Jeremiah has been called, for many centuries, the Weeping Prophet. His story is one that needs to be considered as an example of the price that might be paid to remain faithful to the Father, faithful to the Bible and eventually faithful to the Church. "His road was to become rougher and his suffering greater."[2] Jeremiah's ministry lasted over the reigns of the several Kings of Judah worthy of mention: Josiah, Jehoiakim, Zedekiah and Gedaliah as well as in Egypt, roughly from 627 through 550 BC.

During Jeremiah's prophetic years, Israel had already been taken into captivity as a result of their apostasy, defined as a total departure from one's religion.

When you tell these people all this and they ask you, "Why has the LORD decreed such a great disaster against us? What wrong have we done? What sin have we committed against the LORD our God?" then say to them, "It is because your ancestors forsook me," declares the LORD, "and followed other gods and served and worshiped them. They forsook me and did not keep my law. But you have behaved more wickedly than your ancestors. See how all of you are following the stubbornness of your evil hearts instead of obeying me. So I will throw you out of this land into a land neither you nor your ancestors have known, and there you will serve other gods day and night, for I will show you no favor." (Jeremiah 16:10-13)

Israel had betrayed their blessed relationship with the Lord by following other gods, over many centuries, since the Egyptian experience of slavery and release through the ministry of Moses and Joshua. This behaviour was known as apostasy. God has selected Israel for a purpose, which we will discover afresh, later in this book.

Also notice a particular phrasing in verse 13. There is a clever play on words, in the Hebrew, within this prophetic word. The meaning of the name Jeremiah in Hebrew is 'to hurl'. In this text the Lord told Jeremiah that Judah will be 'hurled' out of this promised land into another land that is foreign, "I will throw you out of this land". Of course, that is what eventually occurred. The actions that describe their leaving, as noted in the prophecy of Jeremiah, were drastic, forceful and confirmed by the eventual results.

Israel is also being accused by Jeremiah of idolatry

Who is wise enough to understand this? Who has been instructed by the Lord and can explain it? Why has the land been ruined and laid waste like a desert that no one can cross? The Lord said, "It is because they have forsaken my law, which I set before them; they have not obeyed me or followed my law. Instead, they have followed the stubbornness of their hearts; they have followed the Baals, as their ancestors taught them." Therefore this is what the Lord Almighty, the God of Israel, says: "See, I will make this people eat bitter food and drink poisoned water. I will scatter them among nations that neither they nor their ancestors have known, and I will pursue them with the sword until I have made an end of them." (Jeremiah 9:12-16; see also 10:1-4, 8-10 and 2:1-9);

Or,

Hear what the Lord says to you, people of Israel. This is what the Lord says:

> Like a scarecrow in a cucumber field,
>   their idols cannot speak;
> they must be carried
>   because they cannot walk.
> Do not fear them;
>   they can do no harm
> nor can they do any good." (Jeremiah 10:5)

Israel had been creating idols, as were other nations around them but Jeremiah indicated they were useless. God had given Israel, much earlier, a purpose of 'telling their world Who He is'. At this time, Judah herself could still be saved from captivity to Babylon and this command would still be upon Judah. Jeremiah prophesied over many decades the message of repentance. Over time he repeated that God would forgive Judah if repentance was evident amongst them.

> This is the word that came to Jeremiah from the Lord: "Listen to the terms of this covenant and tell them to the people of Judah and to those who live in Jerusalem. Tell them that this is what the Lord, the God of Israel, says: 'Cursed is the one who does not obey the terms of this covenant—the terms I commanded your ancestors when I brought them out of Egypt, out of the iron-smelting furnace.' I said, 'Obey me and do everything I command you, and you will be my people, and I will be your God. Then I will fulfill the oath I swore to your ancestors, to give them a land flowing with milk and honey'—the land you possess today'. I answered, "Amen, Lord." (Jeremiah 11:1-5; see also Jeremiah 7:1-7)

And,

But look, you are trusting in deceptive words that are worthless.'" (Jeremiah 7:8)

The phrase 'deceptive words' used here refer to all the false prophets also available to Judah in those years. For example:

A horrible and shocking thing
   has happened in the land:
The prophets prophesy lies,
   the priests rule by their own authority,
and my people love it this way.
   But what will you do in the end? (Jeremiah 5:30-31; see also Jeremiah 23:9-10);

Or,

And you, Pashhur, and all who live in your house will go into exile to Babylon. There you will die and be buried, you and all your friends to whom you have prophesied lies." (Jeremiah 20:6)

Or,

Both prophet and priest are godless;
   even in my temple I find their wickedness,"
     declares the Lord. (Jeremiah 23:11)

Verse 11 refers to one of the most penetrating analyses of true/false prophecy in the Bible. Jeremiah is told by the Lord what false prophets are doing, even as he tried to reach Judah with the Lord's words. (see also Jeremiah 14:13-16; and Jeremiah 26:1-6)

The prophetic message, for Jeremiah, became one of proclaiming the threat of captivity and the destruction of Jerusalem by foreign powers brought to that site by the Lord, Himself.

Jeremiah continued to challenge Israel regarding lies being told by false prophets. All during the years of Jeremiah's prophetic ministry others who were false prophets were proclaiming another story, that Jerusalem would not fall to foreign powers. They were eventually dealt with, by the Lord. Such was the example of the false prophet

Hananiah found in Jeremiah 28:1-4,

> In the fifth month of that same year, the fourth year, early in the reign of Zedekiah king of Judah, the prophet Hananiah son of Azzur, who was from Gibeon, said to me in the house of the Lord in the presence of the priests and all the people: "This is what the Lord Almighty, the God of Israel, says: 'I will break the yoke of the king of Babylon. Within two years I will bring back to this place all the articles of the Lord's house that Nebuchadnezzar king of Babylon removed from here and took to Babylon. I will also bring back to this place Jehoiachin son of Jehoiakim king of Judah and all the other exiles from Judah who went to Babylon,' declares the Lord, 'for I will break the yoke of the king of Babylon.'"

Jeremiah was wearing a yoke he had placed on himself at the time.

Early in the reign of Zedekiah son of Josiah king of Judah, this word came to Jeremiah from the Lord,

> This is what the Lord said to me: "Make a yoke out of straps and crossbars and put it on your neck. Then send word to the kings of Edom, Moab, Ammon, Tyre and Sidon through the envoys who have come to Jerusalem to Zedekiah king of Judah. Give them a message for their masters and say, 'This is what the Lord Almighty, the God of Israel, says: "Tell this to your masters: With my great power and outstretched arm I made the earth and its people and the animals that are on it, and I give it to anyone I please. Now I will give all your countries into the hands of my servant Nebuchadnezzar king of Babylon; I will make even the wild animals subject to him. All nations will serve him and his son and his grandson until the time for his land comes; then many nations and great kings will subjugate him. "'If, however, any nation or kingdom will not serve Nebuchadnezzar king of Babylon or bow its neck under his yoke, I will punish that nation with the sword, famine and plague, declares the Lord, until I destroy it by his hand. So do not listen to your prophets, your

diviners, your interpreters of dreams, your mediums or your sorcerers who tell you, 'You will not serve the king of Babylon.' They prophesy lies to you that will only serve to remove you far from your lands; I will banish you and you will perish. But if any nation will bow its neck under the yoke of the king of Babylon and serve him, I will let that nation remain in its own land to till it and to live there, declares the Lord.'" (Jeremiah 27:1-11)

At the time of this prophecy given by Hananiah, the yoke, which was previously only worn by animals, represented the idea that Judah must put a yoke on itself representing the symbol of submission to Nebuchadnezzar of Babylon.[3] After Hananiah's prophecy indicating among other things that the precious articles taken from the Lord's house would be returned within two years, Jeremiah challenged it. He indicated that a prophecy of peace will be recognized only if it comes true. "But the prophet who prophesies peace will be recognized as one truly sent by the Lord only if his prediction comes true." (Jeremiah 28:9).

Hananiah then responded by breaking the yoke off Jeremiah's neck saying: "this is what the Lord says: 'In the same way I will break the yoke of Nebuchadnezzar king of Babylon off the neck of all the nations within two years'" (Jeremiah 28:10-11). To cut to the chase, "in the seventh month of that same year, Hananiah the prophet died" (Jeremiah 28:17). We will consider further proofs of prophecy later, in this book.

In spite of the terrible prophecies made against a rebellious Judah, the Lord through the prophets, continued to assure Israel that one day they would return to the promised land. "However, the days are coming," declares the Lord, "when it will no longer be said, 'As surely as the Lord lives, who brought the Israelites up out of Egypt,' but it will be said, 'As surely as the Lord lives, who brought the Israelites up out of the land of the north and out of all the countries where he had banished them. 'For I will restore them to the land I gave their ancestors.'" (Jeremiah 16:14-15).

The main thrust of introducing Jeremiah, as well as some other examples following, is that there is a price to pay for faithfulness in declaring the Lord's message to Israel, Judah and eventually to humanity overall. Jeremiah's story is one that, while truthful and exacting, is nevertheless desperately discouraging. Jeremiah is threatened by Judah's leaders.

> Because the Lord revealed their plot to me, I knew it, for at that time he showed me what they were doing. (Jeremiah 11:18; see also Jeremiah 11:19-23)

Further, Jeremiah was asked by the Lord not to marry.

> Then the word of the Lord came to me: "You must not marry and have sons or daughters in this place." For this is what the Lord says about the sons and daughters born in this land and about the women who are their mothers and the men who are their fathers: "They will die of deadly diseases. They will not be mourned or buried but will be like dung lying on the ground. They will perish by sword and famine, and their dead bodies will become food for the birds and the wild animals." (Jeremiah 16:1-4)

He never did marry.

He was also restricted from social practices because of the deteriorating living situation Judah would experience, as they were punished for disobeying the Lord.

> Both high and low will die in this land. They will not be buried or mourned, and no one will cut themselves or shave their head for the dead. For this is what the Lord Almighty, the God of Israel, says: Before your eyes and in your days I will bring an end to the sounds of joy and gladness and to the voices of bride and bridegroom in this place. (Jeremiah 16:6, 9; see also Jeremiah 16:7-8)

Jeremiah's early response to the Lord's call on his life was regret and complaining.

> You deceived me, Lord, and I was deceived;

you overpowered me and prevailed.
I am ridiculed all day long;
　everyone mocks me.
Whenever I speak, I cry out
　proclaiming violence and destruction.
So the word of the Lord has brought me
　insult and reproach all day long.
But if I say, "I will not mention his word
　or speak anymore in his name,"
his word is in my heart like a fire,
　a fire shut up in my bones.
I am weary of holding it in;
　indeed, I cannot.
I hear many whispering,
　"Terror on every side!
　Denounce him! Let's denounce him!"
All my friends
　are waiting for me to slip, saying,
"Perhaps he will be deceived;
　then we will prevail over him
　and take our revenge on him." (Jeremiah 20:7-10)

And,

Cursed be the day I was born!
　May the day my mother bore me not be blessed!
Cursed be the man who brought my father the news,
　who made him very glad, saying,
　"A child is born to you—a son!" (Jeremiah 20:14-15; see also Jeremiah 20:16-18)

He regretted his birth. "Alas, my mother, that you gave me birth, a man with whom the whole land strives and contends! I have neither lent nor borrowed, yet everyone curses me" (Jeremiah 15:10).

He was beaten and put into stocks "When the priest Pashhur son of Immer, the official in charge of the temple of the Lord, heard Jeremiah prophesying these things, he had Jeremiah the prophet beaten and put in the stocks at the Upper Gate of Benjamin at the Lord's temple" (Jeremiah 20:1-2), after which the Lord, through Jeremiah once he was quickly released, gave another but consistent prophecy to the temple priest Pashhur, who had had him beaten. (See Jeremiah 20:3-6).

He nevertheless continued to prophesy the same message, given to him by the Lord at the commencement of his prophetic role, to Jerusalem. So, he was threatened with the taking of his life, by the temple priests and the false prophets of the time.

> Then the priests and the prophets said to the officials and all the people, "This man should be sentenced to death because he has prophesied against this city. You have heard it with your own ears!" (Jeremiah 26:11; see also Jeremiah 26:7-10)

But then they recanted when Jeremiah responded with a challenge that he was open to their deceitful and murderous ideas but God would prevail, nonetheless.

> Then Jeremiah said to all the officials and all the people: "The Lord sent me to prophesy against this house and this city all the things you have heard. Now reform your ways and your actions and obey the Lord your God. Then the Lord will relent and not bring the disaster he has pronounced against you. As for me, I am in your hands; do with me whatever you think is good and right. Be assured, however, that if you put me to death, you will bring the guilt of innocent blood on yourselves and on this city and on those who live in it, for in truth the Lord has sent me to you to speak all these words in your hearing." Then the officials and all the people said to the priests and the prophets, "This man should not be sentenced to death! He has spoken to us in the name of the Lord our God." (Jeremiah 26:12-16)

This back and forth dialogue occurs throughout the book of Jeremiah.

As the years passed Jeremiah continued to be threatened and controlled because of his faithfulness proclaiming the Word of the

Lord to Judah. His life was not his own. On one occasion, during the reign of Jehoiakim king of Judah, Jeremiah was asked by the Lord to write all the words he had received from the Lord, from the reign of Josiah until the present. "Take a scroll and write on it all the words I have spoken to you concerning Israel, Judah and all the other nations from the time I began speaking to you in the reign of Josiah till now" (Jeremiah 36:2). He was asked to put them onto a scroll and give them to Baruch to read in the court of the temple. Jeremiah was kept from coming to the temple court at that time, by the current king. Having done so, Baruch was asked to give the scroll over and the words were then read before the King, who went on to burn the documents as they were read.

> Whenever Jehudi had read three or four columns of the scroll, the king cut them off with a scribe's knife and threw them into the firepot, until the entire scroll was burned in the fire. The king and all his attendants who heard all these words showed no fear, nor did they tear their clothes; Instead, the king commanded Jerahmeel, a son of the king, Seraiah son of Azriel and Shelemiah son of Abdeel to arrest Baruch the scribe and Jeremiah the prophet. But the Lord had hidden them. (Jeremiah 36:23-4; 26)

So once again Jeremiah was to be arrested for his faithfulness to the Lord's request that he prophesy. He continued to not "compromise his conscience".[4]

Later Jeremiah was arrested leaving Jerusalem, while the city was under siege. A new, but weaker king of Judah, Zedekiah, had been inquiring of Jeremiah what the Lord was planning regarding the burning down of the city. Jeremiah continued to give the same dire prophecy.

> Then King Zedekiah sent for him and had him brought to the palace, where he asked him privately, "Is there any word from the Lord?" "Yes," Jeremiah replied, "you will be delivered into the hands of the king of Babylon." (Jeremiah 37:17; see also Jeremiah 37:6-8)

Jeremiah was released and apparently Zedekiah was pleased again.

Some time later, upon leaving the city for personal reasons, Jeremiah was arrested and placed in prison. Zedekiah sent for him and eased his imprisonment by placing him in the courtyard of the guard. "King Zedekiah then gave orders for Jeremiah to be placed in the courtyard of the guard and given a loaf of bread from the street of the bakers each day until all the bread in the city was gone. So Jeremiah remained in the courtyard of the guard" (Jeremiah 37:21).

At this point Jeremiah continued to give further clarification of the picture of the future of Jerusalem. "This is what the Lord says: 'Whoever stays in this city will die by the sword, famine or plague, but whoever goes over to the Babylonians will live. They will escape with their lives; they will live.' And this is what the Lord says: 'This city will certainly be given into the hands of the army of the king of Babylon, who will capture it'" (Jeremiah 38:2-3).

As the tragic story of a faithful prophet of the Lord continues, frustrated and angry officials of a weakened king of Judah placed Jeremiah in a cistern. "So they took Jeremiah and put him into the cistern of Malkijah, the king's son, which was in the courtyard of the guard. They lowered Jeremiah by ropes into the cistern; it had no water in it, only mud, and Jeremiah sank down into the mud" (Jeremiah 38:6).

After a non-Israelite in the king's palace heard of the treatment of Jeremiah, he went to the king in protest.

But Ebed-Melek, a Cushite, an official in the royal palace, heard that they had put Jeremiah into the cistern. While the king was sitting in the Benjamin Gate, Ebed-Melek went out of the palace and said to him, "My lord the king, these men have acted wickedly in all they have done to Jeremiah the prophet. They have thrown him into a cistern, where he will starve to death when there is no longer any bread in the city." Then the king commanded Ebed-Melek the Cushite, "Take thirty men from here with you and lift Jeremiah the prophet out of the cistern before he dies" (Jeremiah 38:7-10).

As Jeremiah's story of faithfulness continues, the Lord uses a non-Israelite to care for Jeremiah's needs. God is above all peoples as he cares for His faithful, throughout the Bible witness. A New Testament example of this same caring of the Father for all peoples is seen in Luke. The Biblical witness to all people is seen in this story. (See Luke 10:29-37). Known by many as 'The Good Samaritan' it is just such an example. A non-Israelite comes to care for a Jew in difficulty.

Later in this story, as Jerusalem falls, Jeremiah receives a prophecy for Ebed-Melek 'because of his trust in the Lord of Judah and Israel. While Jeremiah had been confined in the courtyard of the guard, the word of the Lord came to him, "Go and tell Ebed-Melek the Cushite, 'This is what the Lord Almighty, the God of Israel, says: I am about to fulfill my words against this city—words concerning disaster, not prosperity. At that time they will be fulfilled before your eyes. But I will rescue you on that day, declares the Lord; you will not be given into the hands of those you fear. I will save you; you will not fall by the sword but will escape with your life, because you trust in me, declares the Lord'" (Jeremiah 39:15-18).

Zedekiah reversed that severe reaction and placed him back in the courtyard of the guard. "Ebed-Melek the Cushite said to Jeremiah, 'Put these old rags and worn-out clothes under your arms to pad the ropes.' Jeremiah did so, and they pulled him up with the ropes and lifted him out of the cistern. And Jeremiah remained in the courtyard of the guard" (Jeremiah 38:12-13). The relationship between Jeremiah and Zedekiah continued cordial, even secretive. However, as time went on Jerusalem was eventually captured and burned. Jeremiah, prophet of the Lord, was not given his freedom. "And Jeremiah remained in the courtyard of the guard until the day Jerusalem was captured" (Jeremiah 38:28). He continued as a suffering servant of the Lord.

The army of the king of Babylon did capture Jerusalem and carried off those who remained in the city. However, Nebuchadnezzar inquired of Jeremiah and eventually left him to remain in his own community. Now Nebuchadnezzar king of Babylon had given these orders about Jeremiah through Nebuzaradan commander of the imperial guard,

> Take him and look after him; don't harm him but do for him whatever he asks." So Nebuzaradan the commander of the guard, Nebushazban a chief officer, Nergal-Sharezer a high official and all the other officers of the king of Babylon sent and had Jeremiah taken out of the courtyard of the guard. They turned him over to Gedaliah son of Ahikam, the son of Shaphan, to take him back to his home. So he remained among his own people. (Jeremiah 39:11-14; see also Jeremiah 40:5-6);

The story of Jeremiah's life and prophetic ministry had not ended even at this point, when Jerusalem fell. There was still more prophetic work for Jeremiah. Jews who were a remnant of Judah, still remaining in Israel who had killed the Babylonian, appointed a head of Judah, Gedaliah. They then approached Jeremiah for a further prophecy from the Lord.

> Then all the army officers, including Johanan son of Kareah and Jezaniah son of Hoshaiah, and all the people from the least to the greatest approached Jeremiah the prophet and said to him, "Please hear our petition and pray to the Lord your God for this entire remnant. For as you now see, though we were once many, now only a few are left. Pray that the Lord your God will tell us where we should go and what we should do." Jeremiah 42:1-3)

They indicated they would obey the Lord's word. Then they said to Jeremiah, "May the Lord be a true and faithful witness against us if we do not act in accordance with everything the Lord your God sends you to tell us. Whether it is favorable or unfavorable, we will obey the Lord our God, to whom we are sending you, so that it will go well with us, for we will obey the Lord our God" (Jeremiah 42:5-6). You will again notice subtleties of the story as the Holy Spirit allows us in on the drama. These who were part of the remnant of Judah and giving Jeremiah instructions were not really committed to the Lord. They continue to speak to Jeremiah about **his** God, not theirs. (see verses 2,3,5) But in verse 6, He becomes **their** God. This process, which all of us might consider, did not appear to be sincere and eventually they disobey the Lord, anyway.

Jeremiah did seek the Lord and 10 days later indicated that this remnant must remain in Israel and not go to Egypt, which they were considering doing to be in a perceived safer country in which to locate. He reported on behalf of the Lord:

> Then hear the word of the Lord, you remnant of Judah. This is what the Lord Almighty, the God of Israel, says: "If you are determined to go to Egypt and you do go to settle there, then the sword you fear will overtake you there, and the famine you dread will follow you into Egypt, and there you will die. Indeed, all who are determined to go to Egypt to settle there will die by the sword, famine and plague; not one of them will survive or escape the disaster I will bring on them." (Jeremiah 42:15-17; see also Jeremiah 42:10-14)

But in the end, nothing really changed. The Lord continued to give hope through a faithful prophet Jeremiah, even to the remnant of Judah. Prophecy was clear and effective. This inquiring remnant disobeyed however, once again. Taking Jeremiah with them they left for Egypt. (See Jeremiah 43:4-7).

In 44:28 Jeremiah who continued his role as a prophet to Judah, in Egypt, summarized: the remnant of Judah who came to Egypt will eventually know, through the Father's record in the Bible, "whose word will stand—mine or theirs". Of course, the Bible makes clear throughout Jeremiah and within the other prophesies of the Old and New Testament that the Lord's Word will always stand. Even today, as we shall come to see, the Word of the Lord stands as does no other written or oral tradition, over the many millennia of humanity.

Within the book of Jeremiah are classic themes of restoration. In spite of the idolatry of Judah and Israel, in spite of the fulfillment of the absolutely terrible prophecies from the Lord, there are moments of hope. One theme is found in chapter 32. Jeremiah is challenged, while he was being kept in prison for a brief time by King Zedekiah who was terribly angry at the ongoing prophesy, to buy a field at Anathoth. His cousin Hanamel carried out the deed of selling the field to Jeremiah, at his request. The sale was witnessed and legally carried out even though Jeremiah was a prisoner. He instructed the deed to be placed in a clay jar and buried.

> Then Jeremiah prayed. 'After I had given the deed of purchase to Baruch son of Neriah, I prayed to the Lord: "Ah, Sovereign Lord, you have made the heavens and the earth by your great power and outstretched arm. Nothing is too hard for you. You show love to thousands but bring the punishment for the parents' sins into the laps of their children after them. Great and mighty God, whose name is the Lord Almighty, great are your purposes and mighty are your deeds. Your eyes are open to the ways of all mankind; you reward each person according to their conduct and as their deeds deserve. You performed signs and wonders in Egypt and have continued them to this day, in Israel and among all mankind, and have gained the renown that is still yours. You brought your people Israel out of Egypt with signs and wonders, by a mighty hand and an outstretched arm and with great terror. You gave them this land you had sworn to give their ancestors, a land flowing with milk and honey. They came in and took possession of it, but they did not obey you or follow your law; they did not do what you commanded them to do. So you brought all this disaster on them. "See how the siege ramps are built up to take the city. Because of the sword, famine and plague, the city will be given into the hands of the Babylonians who are attacking it. What you said has happened, as you now see. And though the city will be given into the hands of the Babylonians, you, Sovereign Lord, say to me, 'Buy the field with silver and have the transaction witnessed'". (Jeremiah 32:16-25)

Jeremiah continues to be affirmed by the Lord throughout the experiences of his life, as a called prophet. He paid the price of faithfulness to the Word of the Lord in the context of his ministry.

He here summarized the current situation and the promise that eventually Israel would return and once again build, live and rejoice under the Lord's blessing. God's faithfulness never ends. Jeremiah again quotes: "For this is what the Lord Almighty, the God of Israel, says: Houses, fields and vineyards will again be bought in this land" (Jeremiah 32:15); and then, "I will surely gather them from all the lands where I banish them in my furious anger and great wrath; I will bring them back to this place and let them live in safety" (Jeremiah 32:37).

Jeremiah never returned to Judah after being captured, once again, and taken to Egypt by the Judean remnant. While his death is not recorded in the book, he continued to give prophecy in Egypt. Extrabiblical sources suggest he was stoned to death in Egypt by an angry Judean mob. Over his life, he appears to have been controlled and punished many times. However, he was faithful to the Lord to the end. His life was not one of victory in the way he would have desired but his desire, after having been 'called', became one of serving the Lord, faithfully. In that he was victorious. That is how the Bible describes his life. That is how the Holy Spirit desires that we remember Jeremiah. "Next to Jesus, he was the most successful 'failure' of biblical days, and in many ways, the most Jesus-like man in the Old Testament".[5] He is the first of several biblical characters that paid a heavy price for being faithful to the Lord's call on their lives.

HOSEA

When thinking of prophets who were faithful to God's call on their life and paid a price for that faithfulness, Hosea also comes to mind. Hosea was faithful to the Father's call and is considered a significant prophet in the life of Israel and Judah. He was likely known of by Jeremiah and it is believed Jeremiah was influenced by Hosea's life and ministry. One commentator on Hosea wrote, "Seldom is the revelation of God mediated through such depth of personal anguish and suffering as one finds in Hosea's agony."[6] Hosea's prophecy is most understood through the concept of fidelity. His contribution to the biblical story is significant for Israel and eventually for all who are unfaithful to the living God, by one means or another.

As an introduction to his writings we read, "The word of the Lord that came to Hosea son of Beeri during the reigns of Uzziah, Jotham, Ahaz and Hezekiah, kings of Judah, and during the reign of Jeroboam son of Jehoash king of Israel" (Hosea 1:1). This puts a timeline on the work and writing of Hosea. He lived before Israel was captured and moved into exile. As with other biblical prophets, Hosea came to understand the complexity of preaching the Word of the Lord. 'Hosea's ministry was grounded in the assumption that what God spoke *through* him was predicated upon the fact that God had first spoken *to* him. Dietrich Bonhoeffer once wrote: "I could not preach if I did not know that I speak God's word - and, I could not preach if I did not know that I cannot speak God's word. Human impossibility and Divine promise are one".[7]

Hosea preached a significant message of unfaithfulness by Israel and Judah to the God of their fathers. To seek to communicate to the people of the time, his prophecy was captured and understood by the personal experience of unfaithfulness. Hosea was the first among the prophets to use the figure of marriage to symbolize the relationship between Israel and the Lord, Yahweh. Later Jeremiah used the same symbology.

> The word of the Lord came to me: "Go and proclaim in the hearing of Jerusalem:
>
> This is what the Lord says:
>
>> 'I remember the devotion of your youth,
>> how as a bride you loved me
>> and followed me through the wilderness,
>> through a land not sown. (Jeremiah 2:1-2)
>
> And again,

> If a man divorces his wife
> and she leaves him and marries another man,
> should he return to her again?
> Would not the land be completely defiled?
> But you have lived as a prostitute with many lovers—
> would you now return to me?"
> declares the Lord. (Jeremiah 3:1)

Infidelity fractures the bonds of faithfulness in a marriage. In this prophecy the fracturing of the covenant relationship with the Lord over time is symbolized for Israel by the life of the marriage of Hosea and Gomer. Through the prophet's life of marriage, the Israelites could more clearly come to understand the deterioration of their relationship to the Lord, as Hosea prophesied to them.

Hosea was asked by the Lord, through the Holy Spirit, to marry a woman who, in all likelihood given the character of God, was a virgin at the time of their marriage but shortly became promiscuous and an adulterer. That this unfaithfulness would occur was known by the Lord. Through Hosea's experience and prophecy, Israel was being accused by the Lord of disloyalty to the Covenant made with Abraham and his descendants. The promises of blessing given to Israel by the Lord were now jeopardized by their behavior, over generations, since being freed from Egypt. By the time of Hosea "the people of God had abandoned the Lord, the source of meaning and order and sought that order and blessing from Baal."[8]

Hosea's life as a prophet rendered him pain, suffering and tragedy over the years of his marriage and child bearing. "Seldom is the revelation of God mediated through such depth of personal anguish and suffering as one finds in Hosea's agony".[9] The call on his life, by the Lord, to speak to Israel was clear and he responded.

> When the Lord began to speak through Hosea, the Lord said to him, "Go, marry a promiscuous woman and have children with her, for like an adulterous wife this land is guilty of unfaithfulness to the Lord." Hosea named his first son Jezreel. So he married Gomer daughter of Diblaim, and she conceived and

bore him a son. Then the Lord said to Hosea, "Call him Jezreel, because I will soon punish the house of Jehu for the massacre at Jezreel, and I will put an end to the kingdom of Israel. In that day I will break Israel's bow in the Valley of Jezreel." (Hosea 1: 2-5)

The name Jezreel would first remind Israel of a successful battle had by Jehu as seen in 2 Kings 9-10. However by the time of Hosea's prophecy, Israel having lived through much tragic battle history over that same valley would view the name with distain. The name of the prophet's son would be seen as a haunting indictment. "Like some ghostly apparition Hosea's son recalled for his generation the darkened fields of the valley and the blood-flecked streets of the ancient village of Jezreel."[10] In naming this first son Jezreel, Hosea was demonstrating the embodiment of his personal agony.

Gomer conceived a second time and gave birth to a daughter. Gomer conceived again and gave birth to a daughter. Then the Lord said to Hosea, "Call her Lo-Ruhamah (which means "not loved"), for I will no longer show love to Israel, that I should at all forgive them. Yet I will show love to Judah; and I will save them—not by bow, sword or battle, or by horses and horsemen, but I, the Lord their God, will save them." (Hosea 1:6-7)

According to this prophecy, in part, the Lord asked Hosea to give her a name 'not pitied' meaning 'I will no longer show love to Israel'. Again, Hosea was giving a message to Israel through his personal pain, his personal life. The Lord was also passing on this message to Israel, His chosen bride through the prophecy, that He will no longer love them as He has in the ancient past. A personal relationship with the Lord, which Israel had forsaken, was then and still is crucial throughout an understanding of the Bible and written prophecy then and now. However, as the story of Israel/Judah developed over the centuries, Judah was given another way to deal with their spiritual adultery and idolatry, as per verse 7 above.

Their third child, a son, was to be named 'not my people'. After she had weaned Lo-Ruhamah, Gomer had another son. "Then the

Lord said, 'Call him Lo-Ammi (which means "not my people"), for you are not my people, and I am not your God'" (Hosea 1:8-9). While some commentators have suggested the name could mean that Hosea was not sure he was the father of this child, as in actual adultery, it is pushing the Hebrew text to suggest this was actually the case. However, the use of this name choice by the Lord clearly means that this son represents, 'I am not your God and you are no longer my people'. The Lord is moving His love and blessing away from Israel, through the birth of these three children. The phrase "...I will be their God and they shall be my people" (Ezekiel 37:27) was clearly understood by Israel, as ancient covenant language. This child's name represents the complete disruption of covenant life, for Israel.

Following the birth of Hosea and Gomer's three children, all demonstrating the involvement of the Lord in their experiences, particularly for the benefit of Israel, Hosea prophesies a further message from the Lord. He is asked by the Lord to reconcile with Gomer.

> The Lord said to me, "Go, show your love to your wife again, though she is loved by another man and is an adulteress. Love her as the Lord loves the Israelites, though they turn to other gods and love the sacred raisin cakes." So I bought her for fifteen shekels of silver and about a homer and a lethek of barley. Then I told her, "You are to live with me many days; you must not be a prostitute or be intimate with any man, and I will behave the same way toward you." (Hosea 3:1-3)

It was the purpose of the prophet's message, under the influence of the Holy Spirit, to bring Gomer to a place of eventual redemption and forgiveness. It involved a cost and a commitment on the part of both of them.

These birth experiences became a prophetic message, as well. The life of tragedy, when completed and redeemed, was further used by the prophet Hosea to suggest to Israel that as bad as things had become between them and the Lord, there is always hope for a future and an eventual reconciliation. The clarity of this message given to

Israel took place by way of a purchase, by Hosea, of his wife Gomer, who was by then living as a prostitute. There was a significant cost to the purchase. (3:2 above) Hosea had Gomer commit to sexual faithfulness as well as committing the same for himself. Hosea went on to catalogue the sins of Israel and her need for reconciliation. Throughout the Bible the message is clear that forgiveness and restoration are costly and yet always possible. Eventually, centuries later, that cost would be borne by the birth, life, ministry, death and resurrection of Jesus.

The pain and loss to Hosea, and no doubt to Gomer, was clearly evident as the years of his ministry and eventually 'their' ministry passed. "Only the later suffering of Jesus transcends the personal sorrow of Hosea as a medium of divine revelation."[11] Therefore, as well as Jeremiah, we have found that the price of following the leading of the Father can be costly. "Heartache and alienation were all too often the sad accompaniments of both Hosea and Jesus." "But more than this they shared the bond of a common identification with sorrow as the vehicle of ministry"-- Hosea and Jesus. Another commentator, Wheeler Robinson, referred to the prophet's message under the title 'The Cross of Hosea'.[12] Such is the grand design of the Lord's purpose in giving us the Bible. There is always the 'last chapter'. There have been others as well who have been faithful and paid the price.

JOHN, THE BAPTIZER

Another character in the Bible who demonstrated faithfulness to the Lord's leading in their life was John the baptizer. Often referred to by English translators as John the Baptist, he was not a Baptist as that group of believers identified themselves by the description of 'Baptist', centuries later. John was baptizing, hence 'the Baptizer'. John's story of pain and suffering is briefly described in the New Testament.

However, the prophecy concerning him, according to the Bible, is found in Isaiah 40. The prophet, in order to bring comfort to Israel at the time, gave a prophecy regarding one who would come as 'as voice in the wilderness'.

> A voice of one calling:
> "In the wilderness prepare
>   the way for the Lord,
> make straight in the desert
>   a highway for our God.
> Every valley shall be raised up,
>   every mountain and hill made low;
> the rough ground shall become level,
>   the rugged places a plain.
> And the glory of the Lord will be revealed,
>   and all people will see it together.
> For the mouth of the Lord has spoken." (Isaiah 40:3-5)

The Gospel writers, centuries later, referred to Isaiah's words and suggested that John the baptizer was the fulfillment of this encouraging prophecy. Later, reference will be made as to the significance of prophecy, within the Bible.

John's life is introduced and described in each of the four gospels. Such is the importance of his life and ministry as the early church is about to be established. "In those days John the Baptist came, preaching in the wilderness of Judea" (Matthew 3:1). He was called as a preacher and he came from the 'outside' of society at the time, 'preaching in the wilderness'. There is little reference to John's personal life in the Bible. We do not know whether or not he married, had children, or had an ongoing and consistent relationship with his parents. His birth and lineage are described in Luke's Gospel.

> In the time of Herod king of Judea there was a priest named Zechariah, who belonged to the priestly division of Abijah; his wife Elizabeth was also a descendant of Aaron. Both of them were righteous in the sight of God, observing all the Lord's commands and decrees blamelessly. But they were childless because Elizabeth was not able to conceive, and they were both very old. (Luke 1:5-7)

Barrenness was understood as a 'curse' at this time in the history of Israel and Elizabeth had not had any children in her old age. Luke's account of John's birth brings significance to John's life. "After this his wife Elizabeth became pregnant and for five months remained in seclusion. "The Lord has done this for me," she said. "In these days he has shown his favor and taken away my disgrace among the people" (Luke 1:24-25); and "When it was time for Elizabeth to have her baby, she gave birth to a son. Her neighbors and relatives heard that the Lord had shown her great mercy, and they shared her joy. On the eighth day they came to circumcise the child, and they were going to name him after his father Zechariah, but his mother spoke up and said, "No! He is to be called John" (Luke 1:57-60).

Matthew's gospel described John's ministry and tied it to an Old Testament prophecy, thus recognizing its fulfillment, centuries later. John was preaching and saying, "Repent, for the kingdom of heaven has come near. This is he who was spoken of through the prophet Isaiah: A voice of one calling in the wilderness, 'Prepare the way for the Lord, make straight paths for him'" (Matthew 3:2-3). John was to prepare Israel for the coming of the promised Messiah when repentance was to be required on the part of all of Israel. This message was not popular with religious leaders or any Jews at that time. "But when he saw many of the Pharisees and Sadducees coming to where he was baptizing, he said to them: 'You brood of vipers! Who warned you to flee from the coming wrath?'" (Luke 3:7) He looked the part of a recluse. "John's clothes were made of camel's hair, and he had a leather belt around his waist. His food was locusts and wild honey. People went out to him from Jerusalem and all Judea and the whole region of the Jordan. Confessing their sins, they were baptized by him in the Jordan River" (Matthew 3:4-6). He dressed and ate in the manner of one who was alone but his message was powerful and reverberated with the people.

His ministry was productive. Jews and Gentiles listened to him and heard him; so, he baptized many. His unpopularity with Israel's leadership revolved around his demand for repentance and his call of demanding baptism by immersion. Hebrew tradition included this act but only for proselytes; those who were Gentiles who desired to become Jews. The tragedy of his short-lived ministry, while unpopular with the Pharisees and Sadducees, was not, however, in the end caused by a Jewish leadership decision.

John was faithful to the Lord's call on his life. He was humble. "Then Jesus came from Galilee to the Jordan to be baptized by John. But John tried to deter him, saying, 'I need to be baptized by you, and do you come to me?' Jesus replied, 'Let it be so now; it is proper for us to do this to fulfill all righteousness.' Then John consented" (Matthew 3:13-15).

Jesus also had much to say about John's ministry. In response to John's disciples' queries about Jesus, Jesus challenged them to report to John what they saw. (See Matthew 11:4-15). Jesus indicated John's was a ministry of faithfulness in the midst of challenge and opposition. Jesus affirmed John. He tied him to the prophecies regarding the 'one who would come and be 'the voice of one calling in the wilderness' centuries after that prophecy was proclaimed.

John's untimely and cruel death, by being beheaded, commenced with his being put into prison by King Herod. "When Jesus heard that John had been put in prison, he withdrew to Galilee" (Matthew 4:12; see also Matthew 14:3-11; Mark 1:14). John's imprisonment also was seen as a sign for Jesus to begin his public ministry throughout the region, beginning in Galilee. John had verbally challenged Herod's immoral behavior. Herod wanted to kill John because of the prophet's public criticism of his behavior but he was apparently afraid to kill John, because the Jews considered him a prophet. However, through some trickery by his brother's wife's daughter, at his birthday celebration, Herod had to agree to kill John who would have been a very young man at the time.

JESUS OF NAZARETH

Another biblical figure to consider when looking at those who suffered when they believed God the Father was communicating with them, was Jesus of Nazareth. Jesus, the man, is tied to historical Jewish ancestors. The Gospel of Matthew, chapter one, indicates that Jesus' ancestry is tied to David and Abraham. This was important for Matthew who was Jewish. "Thus there were fourteen generations in all from Abraham to David, fourteen from David to the exile to Babylon, and fourteen from the exile to the Messiah" (Matthew 1:17). Different Gospel writers gave evidence of Jesus' ministry from different perspectives. Dr. Luke, for example, was not Jewish so he wrote for a Greek official. "With this in mind, since I myself have carefully investigated everything from the beginning, I too decided to write an orderly account for you, most excellent Theophilus, so that you may know the certainty of the things you have been taught" (Luke 1:3-4). Luke also writes of Jesus' ancestry in chapter three, as Jesus begins his ministry at about 30 years of age. Both writers clearly emphasize the birth of Jesus and its importance.

From the very beginning of Jesus' life, according to the Bible, he suffered for his eventual obedience to the call of God on His life. One of the first challenges for his parents, because of Who he was, occurred early in his life. His parents had to take him away secretly because of the potential threat to the baby's life. This threat came from King Herod who believed that Jesus' status threatened his kingship.

> When they had gone, an angel of the LORD appeared to Joseph in a dream. "Get up," he said, "take the child and his mother and escape to Egypt. Stay there until I tell you, for Herod is going to search for the child to kill him." So he got up, took the child and his mother during the night and left for Egypt, where he stayed until the death of Herod. And so was fulfilled what the LORD had said through the prophet: "Out of Egypt I called my son." (Matthew 2:13-15)

> Jesus had to flee from home, even as an infant.

> When Jesus was 12, on the annual visit to Jerusalem for Pass-

over, another challenge came to him, because he was obedient to the Father's call on his life. He had remained in the city, at the temple courts, when his parents had left for home at the conclusion of the festivities. Upon returning to look for their son, Joseph and Mary inquired of him why he had not joined them in the return home? He responded, "'Why were you searching for me?' he asked. 'Didn't you know I had to be in my Father's house?' But they did not understand what he was saying to them" (Luke 2:49-50). Jesus had begun to understand the call on His life, the potential of suffering, but it would still be years away. He continued to obey his parents and worked with his father as a carpenter. According to the Bible that purpose came much clearer to him when he was around 30.

As this ministry began Jesus returned to Nazareth where he had been brought up, to the synagogue on the Sabbath which had been his custom. There on that day, according to Luke, Jesus confirmed to the 'world' what he was really about and why he had been born. He was handed a scroll from the prophet Isaiah which was read often. He read, "The Spirit of the LORD is on me, because he has anointed me to proclaim good news to the poor. He has sent me to proclaim freedom for the prisoners and recovery of sight for the blind, to set the oppressed free, to proclaim the year of the LORD's favor" (Luke 4:18-19). This text had always been understood as applying to Isaiah. It was a description of the prophet's ongoing mission to the postexilic community: to those Jews whose captivity had not yet ended. However, on this occasion, Jesus took this important text and changed the meaning. "Then he rolled up the scroll, gave it back to the attendant and sat down. The eyes of everyone in the synagogue were fastened on him. He began by saying to them, 'Today this scripture is fulfilled in your hearing'" (Luke 4:20-21).

Here, Jesus took on the part of the promised Messiah as described in Old Testament writings. The prophet Isaiah described the coming Messiah in what is known as a servant song, of which there are three. He described the experience of that Servant. "I offered my back to those who beat me, my cheeks to those who pulled out my beard; I did not hide my face from mocking and spitting" (Isaiah 50:6). In this passage and many others the prophet, under the influence of the Holy Spirit, describes what will be some of the experiences of that Servant of Israel.

Jesus was aware that he would suffer much by acknowledging this role. His interpretation of these passages here influenced the rest of his earthly life and ministry. He had arrived in a way that confirmed Biblical prophecy, which will later be considered. His ministry became notable within the Jewish community at the time and because of Bible prophecy, became notable worldwide.

For the rest of Jesus' earthly life, he suffered in various ways. From this point on Jesus was followed and challenged by the religious leadership. His popularity with Israel was a consternation to them. His authority to teach was questioned. "Jesus entered the temple courts, and, while he was teaching, the chief priests and the elders of the people came to him. 'By what authority are you doing these things?' they asked. 'And who gave you this authority?'" (Matthew 21:23) The religious leaders of Israel sought to find reason to kill Jesus. They were convinced he was not who he claimed to be and whom the people believed he was. The chief priests and the whole Sanhedrin were looking for evidence against Jesus so that they could put him to death, but they did not find any. (Mark 14:55) But they kept up the pressure over the next several years. "Then the chief priests and the elders of the people assembled in the palace of the high priest, whose name was Caiaphas, and they schemed to arrest Jesus secretly and kill him. 'But not during the festival,' they said, 'or there may be a riot among the people'" (Matthew 26:3-5).

Jesus was betrayed by his closest followers, one of his disciples. Judas, who believed that Jesus was to rescue Israel from Roman dominance, set up a plan to force Jesus' hand. He conspired with Jewish leadership to have Jesus arrested.

While he was still speaking, Judas, one of the Twelve, arrived. With him was a large crowd armed with swords and clubs, sent from the chief priests and the elders of the people. Now the betrayer had arranged a signal with them: "The one I kiss is the man; arrest him." Going at once to Jesus, Judas said, "Greetings, Rabbi!" and kissed him. Jesus replied, "Do what you came for, friend." Then the men stepped forward, seized Jesus and arrested him. (Matthew 26:47-50)

Later, suffering from his own anguish of realizing what he had done and with Jesus not obviously going on to conquer Roman dominance, Judas took his own life by hanging himself.

Jesus was eventually hung on a cross where he physically died. "Jesus called out with a loud voice, 'Father, into your hands I commit my spirit.' When he had said this, he breathed his last" (Luke 23:46). All the Gospel writers refer to the death of Jesus. The man who had believed he was following the Word of the Father to himself, suffered much on a cross and died. "Only the later suffering of Jesus transcends the personal sorrow of Hosea as a medium of divine revelation."[13]

Unique to the telling of His story however, is that according to the Bible, Jesus is alive. All that you have read about Jesus, the historical figure, has occurred to One who rose from the dead, is alive and will someday return according to the Biblical record.

BONHOEFFER

Much more recently the life, ministry and passing on of Dietrich Bonhoeffer fits into the observation of some people, over the millennia, who over their lives sought to come to an understanding of the Father's influence on themselves and the relevance of that understanding to that life lived. Bonhoeffer was born in Germany (1906-1945) and studied to become a theologian and pastor. Although his family and his siblings were not churchgoers, all the children were confirmed at the Grunewald church in Berlin. In the early 1920's, as a teenager, he was influenced spiritually by General Bramwell Booth of the Salvation Army. Also, at that time there was much turmoil in the Weimar Republic. Significant conflicts in his life occurred between the political upheaval in Germany and his developing understanding of the role of the Father in his personal devotional life, his education and his experiences of the church and its leadership.

Over his brief lifetime, Bonhoeffer was well travelled. He travelled to America several times as well as to many countries in Europe. As Hitler began to gain influence in Germany and as he worked to eliminate the influence of the church in a new society, Bonhoeffer was able to move about inside and outside of the country without significant restrictions from the then dominating anti-faith Reich.

In his early years of study, Bonhoeffer came to understand that theology and philosophy were separate and distinct and that the former "begins and ends with faith in Christ, who reveals himself to man; apart from such revelation, there could be no such thing as truth".[14] In *Act and Being* published in 1930 Bonhoeffer wrote,

> The revelation of the Father to humanity 'is a matter of God's given Word, the covenant in which God is bound by God's own action. It is a question of the freedom of God, which finds its strongest evidence precisely in that God freely chose to be bound in historical human beings and to be placed at the disposal of human beings. God is free not from human beings but for them. Christ is the word of God's freedom. God is present... graspable in the Word within the church. Here the formal understanding of God's freedom is countered by a substantial one.' (89-90). As Bonhoeffer studied diligently and worked out his understanding of the revelation of God to humankind over his lifetime, he was able to come to a clear conception of how God, the Father, works though humankind to get tasks accomplished. Our openness to the Father, through the Word and a disciplined personal devotional life can make differences in the world.[15]

That understanding of the relationship between humanity and the Father's desire to communicate with us about who Jesus is, though the Holy Spirit's communication to us all, worked in Bonhoeffer's life to bring to us a simple and yet profound example of this relationship. As Germany was seemingly moving to become more overtaken by

Hitler's political force and his plans for 'real' Germans in that part of Europe, Bonhoeffer went to England as a pastor and preacher, from 1933 to 1935. He became aware more acutely, thorough ongoing correspondence with members of his family in Germany, like a prophet of old, of the potential of the danger of the third Reich. One January Sunday morning, while there, he took a text from the prophecy of Jeremiah. Like the prophet realizing the danger developing in his homeland, he attempted to convince German believers, in England, of the developing catastrophe in their homeland. He wanted to warn them, to have them separate their loyalties. In his recently published book,[16] Metaxas sought to clearly paint a picture of an apparent prophet, realizing that his own future was in jeopardy as he continued to be lovingly 'glued' to his own homeland. There was, for Bonhoeffer, a sense that he was becoming aware of his own future, the future God was showing him. He was seeking to warn believers in England of the coming peril or catastrophe.

Bonhoeffer, over the next years, would wrestle with the awareness of the dangers for the Church, the believers in Germany, and his own desire to be there with them through what apparently could become a very troubled and horrific period of German history. So as one becomes briefly aware of the life of Dietrich Bonhoeffer, it is noticed as well that his choices to follow the leading of the Holy Spirit brought about much pain and eventually an early and tragic death.

There appears to be an unsettledness in his life and study. He wrote much. He posted many a letter which was typical correspondence in the 1930's. He travelled much, as noted earlier, and thus never really had a 'home of his own' except for the traditional residence of his family, his parents and siblings. That apparent 'unsettledness' could have been a by-product of his deepening awareness of the eventual coming horrors of the Nazi regime in Germany and in Europe.

Bonhoeffer was concerned for the Church, worldwide not just in Germany. He so desired to communicate the glory of Christ and the resurrection to eternal life. As he became of age to be drafted, he worked through known associates of the German government, at the time, to become a pastor with a wider ministry than a local pastor in Germany. This enabled him to become a sort of spiritual leader and less likely to be sent to the front. He was not a pacifist but did not want to be a soldier who would take life. It also enabled him to continue study and writing.

One tragic part of his life, briefly, is that of his relationship with Maria von Wedemeyer. They met in June, 1942. She was somewhat younger than he and the family was not enamored with what appeared to be an affection developing between them. Over the course of the next two years they corresponded. They stopped corresponding. They commenced it again. They met several times, for Bonhoeffer was travelling much and would get to her home area, deliberately. She remained at home as the relationship developed slowly and eventually in January, 1943 they were engaged. However, with the obvious political tensions nationally related to Germany's war effort, they decided to wait for an anticipated end of the war to marry. Their frequent letter correspondence was deeply personal. Here was a young couple in love, desiring to marry but, in part, because of the 'underground' role in which Bonhoeffer had been engaged for years, they never married. Marie was mostly aware of his efforts, as well, to plot the death of Hitler. In April of that year he was arrested and remained in prison for the rest of his life; actually, not much more than another year.

In the months just before his arrest, Bonhoeffer had written an essay on an assessment of what he and his political cohort had all been through in the ten years since Hitler's ascension. One can find reference to this material in Metaxas's book on Bonhoeffer.[17] It gives an understanding, to some extent, of the depth of the spiritual maturity evident in Bonhoeffer at that time. He had so come to understand the depth of the Believer's faith in God; also, the price that has, at times, to be paid. Bonhoeffer writes,

If we want to be Christians, we must have some share in Christ's large-heartedness by acting with responsibility and in freedom when the hour of danger comes and by showing a real sympathy that springs, not from fear, but from the liberating and redeeming love of Christ for all who suffer. Mere waiting and looking on is not Christian behaviour. The Christian is called to sympathy and action, not in the first place by his own sufferings, but by the sufferings of his brethren, for whose sake Christ suffered.[18]

So, like the prophet Jeremiah he was arrested, for his resistance which he understood was influenced under the leadership of the Father through the Holy Spirit, by the leadership in his country at the time. Somewhat similar to the prophet Hosea, Bonhoeffer's relationship with the love of his life was tragic, in the end. Bonhoeffer was killed by the Nazis April, 1945 at the request of Hitler, who killed himself just two weeks later as the Second War ended.

Endnotes

1. James Leo Green, *Jeremiah – Daniel*, in The Broadman Bible Commentary, ed. Clifton J. Allen (Nashville: Broadman Press, 1971), Vol 6: 93.
2. Green, *Jeremiah*, 7.
3. Green, *Jeremiah*, 137.
4. Green, Jeremiah, 169.
5. Green, *Jeremiah*, 182.
6. Roy L. Honeycutt, *Hosea*, in The Broadman Bible Commentary, ed. Clifton J. Allen (Nashville: Broadman Press, 1971), Vol 7:1.
7. Honeycutt, *Hosea*, 9-10.
8. Honeycutt, *Hosea*, 4.
9. Honeycutt, *Hosea*, 1.
10. Honeycutt, *Hosea*, 10.
11. Honeycutt, *Hosea*, 1.
12. Honeycutt, *Hosea*, 1.
13. Honeycutt, *Hosea*, 1.
14. Eric Metaxas, *Bonhoeffer: Pastor, Martyr, Prophet, Spy* (Nashville: Thomas Nelson, 2010) 89.
15. Dietrich Bonhoeffer, *Act and Being: Works Vol. 2* (Philadelphia: Fortress Press, 1996; first published 1930).
16. Metaxas, *Bonhoeffer*.
17. Metaxas, *Bonhoeffer*, 445ff.
18. Metaxas, *Bonhoeffer*, 447.

Chapter 3

CRITIQUE OF THE BIBLE'S AUTHORITY OVER THE CENTURIES

Throughout the history of the existence of the written Word of God, many have attempted to challenge this Bible as to its value to humanity overall. Over the centuries, since the Bible was printed and available to the average person who could read, debate about its authenticity and authority has continued. In earlier centuries those familiar with the Latin were versed in the challenges of the authenticity of the Scriptures, the very Word of God to humanity. Various Biblical texts were available from 1400's BC to 1400's AD. The scriptures (Guttenberg Bible, printed in the 1450's) were printed in German. John Wycliffe translated portions of scripture, hand written, from Hebrew, Greek and Latin to English in the 1380's. Although it is impossible to obtain exact figures, there is little doubt that the Bible is the world's best-selling and most widely distributed book. A survey by the Bible Society concluded that around 2.5 billion copies were printed between 1815 and 1975, but more recent estimates put the number at more than 5 billion.

JOHN CALVIN

Amongst several of the theologians who were involved in early biblical criticism was John Calvin (1509-1564). He took up the challenge to the inspiration of the Bible obviously early, even before the work of 19th century biblical criticism. Calvin's view of Scripture is set forth in some passages in the first nine chapters of one of his works The Institutes. In studying Calvin, Kuiper wrote: "It is only after he has laid down the principle of biblical authority that he allows himself and the reader to proceed to a consideration of the doctrines of God, man, Christ, salvation, and the church."[1] Kuiper went on to write: "It is clear, therefore, that Calvin taught that the study of creation by science, although more than sufficient to deprive the ingratitude of men of every excuse, was not sufficient to give anything more than confused notions of deity. There is not, in his view, a reciprocal relation between Scripture and scientific findings by which each cast true light upon the other, as the theistic evolutionist holds today. Calvinists must avoid that proud pitfall and confess that Scripture alone gives us the truth regarding creation and the Creator."

The ongoing tension between the fluid writings of the 'scientific' world and the writings of the Scriptures has continued to this day. While science, as we know it, was born of the study of the Bible, the investigation of our world continues to be encouraged by the Bible. Humanity is curious by nature, God created us thus. But as the prophet considered the comparison between humanity and its curiosity, he challenged us to keep a perspective of Creator and created. "You turn things upside down, as if the potter were thought to be like the clay! Shall what is formed say to the one who formed it, 'You did not make me'? Can the pot say to the potter, 'You know nothing?'" (Isaiah 29:16) Job understood that humans need to search for the benefits of the created world. "There is a mine for silver and a place where gold is refined. Iron is taken from the earth, and copper is smelted from ore. Mortals put an end to the darkness; they search out the farthest recesses for ore in the blackest darkness." (Job 28:1-3) and further,

> People assault the flinty rock with their hands
>   and lay bare the roots of the mountains.
> They tunnel through the rock;
>   their eyes see all its treasures.
> They search the sources of the rivers
>   and bring hidden things to light.
>
> But where can wisdom be found?
>   Where does understanding dwell?
> No mortal comprehends its worth;
>   it cannot be found in the land of the living." (Job 28:9-13)

Or finally,

> Where then does wisdom come from?
>   Where does understanding dwell?
> It is hidden from the eyes of every living thing,
>   concealed even from the birds in the sky.
> Destruction and Death say,
>   "Only a rumor of it has reached our ears."
> God understands the way to it
>   and he alone knows where it dwells,
> for he views the ends of the earth
>   and sees everything under the heavens.
> When he established the force of the wind
>   and measured out the waters,
> when he made a decree for the rain
>   and a path for the thunderstorm,
> then he looked at wisdom and appraised it;
>   he confirmed it and tested it.
> And he said to the human race,
>   "The fear of the Lord—that is wisdom,
>   and to shun evil is understanding." (Job 28:20-28)

So it is with humans who all have a desire to understand the world around; to gain wisdom about our world, it always has been.

The ongoing and changing conclusions from science about the world around us seem to contradict the biblical record, from time to time. But the Scriptures were never intended to be 'scientific' as we have come to know the study. The Scriptures are 'truth' as we shall come to see.

So Calvin, in his Institutes, notes: "But since we are not favoured with daily oracles from heaven, and since it is only in the Scriptures that the Lord hath been pleased to preserve his truth in perpetual remembrance, it obtains the same complete credit and authority with believers, when they are satisfied of its divine origin, as if they heard the very words pronounced by God himself".[2] Calvin believed the Holy Spirit is completely involved with the Bible's creation and ongoing protection.

For Calvin, it was apparent that another affirmation of a faith in Scriptures' validity is the endurance of the Word of God throughout all generations. Himself in awe, he writes, "For it is not an unimportant consideration, that, since the publication of the Scripture, so many generations of humanity should have agreed in voluntarily obeying it; and that however Satan, together with the whole world, has endeavored by strange methods to suppress or destroy it, or utterly to erase and obliterate it from the memory of man, yet it has always, like a palm-tree, risen superior to all opposition, and remained invincible".[3] Calvin ascribes the preserving of Scripture throughout the ages, not to the church or the faithfulness of **humankind**, but to the providence of God. This comforting, historical fact is, for Calvin, proof that the Bible is a Divine Book.

A further proof that can assist our faith in receiving the doctrines of the Bible with confidence is that it has been confirmed by the blood of so many saints. Again, from Calvin, "Having once received it, they hesitated not, with intrepid boldness, and even with great alacrity, to die in its defence: transmitted to us with such a pledge, how should we not receive it with a firm and unshaken conviction? Is it therefore no small confirmation of the Scripture, that it has been sealed with the blood of so many martyrs".[4] As I have noted elsewhere, I have been so impressed with the faith in the Scriptures of people who have, over more recent decades, travelled to parts of the world to those who are living under totalitarian dictatorships and delivered the Bible, in clandestine situations, to the faithful.

Further, Calvin was intolerant of those who pretended not to need the Scripture because they had apparently received special revelations from the Spirit. He called this attempt to separate Word and Spirit ridiculous, puerile, mean, and subversive. "The office of the Spirit, then, which is promised to us, is not to feign new and unheard of revelations, or to coin a new system of doctrine, which would seduce us from the received doctrine of the Gospel, but to seal to our minds the same doctrine which the Gospel delivers".[5] "Since the Spirit is the author of Scripture, He cannot by secret revelations be inconsistent with Himself. He always testifies to His own truth which He has expressed in Scripture, with the result that he only displays and exerts his power where the Word is received with due reverence and piety".[6] I will further refer to some of the problems created by writers in our own day who seek to determine that what is 'truth' about some lifestyle or behaviour conflicts with the revealed Word, given by the Holy Spirit over time.

ROMAN CATHOLIC CHURCH

The Roman Catholic church also was involved with the creation and development of the field of biblical criticism, which had been in play since the 17th century.

Providentissimus Deus, which meant "On the Study of Holy Scripture", was an encyclical letter issued by Pope Leo the VIII on 18 November, 1893. In it, he reviewed the history of Bible study from the time of the Church Fathers to the then present, spoke against the errors of the Rationalists and "higher critics" and outlined principles of scriptural study. He gave guidelines for how scripture was to be taught in seminaries. He also addressed the issues of apparent contradictions between the Bible and physical science, or between one part of scripture and another, and how such apparent contradictions can be resolved. Something similar has been an influence on my reflections over the past years, as well.

Pope Leo also gave the first formal authorization for the use of critical methods in biblical scholarship within the Roman Catholic faith. In 1902, Pope Leo XIII instituted the Pontifical Biblical Commission which was to adapt Roman Catholic Biblical studies to modern scholarship and to protect Scripture against attacks. Leo quoted Augustine: "And if in these Books I meet anything which seems contrary to truth, I shall not hesitate to conclude either that the text is faulty, or that the translator has not expressed the meaning of the passage, or that I myself do not understand" (On the Study of Holy Scriptures, 1893). To suggest that the text is faulty, by which I believe he meant 'in translation', brings into the debate the idea that the Holy Spirit in His work of communicating the Word of God to humanity, might have made a mistake in communication with the faithful writer. He expressed a humility with the idea that he might not understand a text. Our study of the Bible must always go back to the conviction of the security of the work of the Holy Spirit in communicating God's intentions to humankind.

ST. AUGUSTINE

From much earlier, but influential to this consideration of the Authority of the Bible, from St. Augustine one can read,

> Usually, even a non-Christian knows something about the earth, the heavens, and the other elements of this world, about the motion and orbit of the stars and even their size and relative positions, about the predictable eclipses of the sun and moon, the cycles of the years and the seasons, about the kinds of animals, shrubs, stones, and so forth and this knowledge they hold to as being certain from reason and experience. Now, it is a disgraceful and dangerous thing for an infidel to hear a Christian, presumably giving the meaning of Holy Scripture, talking

CRITIQUE OF THE BIBLE'S AUTHORITY OVER THE CENTURIES

non-sense on these topics; and we should take all means to prevent such an embarrassing situation, in which people show up vast ignorance of Christian faith and laugh it to scorn. The shame is not so much that an ignorant individual is derided, but that people outside the household of the faith think our sacred writers held such opinions, and, to the great loss of those for whose salvation we toil, the writers of our Scripture are criticized and rejected as unlearned men and women. If they find a Christian mistaken in a field which they themselves know well and hear him maintaining his foolish opinions about our books, how are they going to believe those books in matters concerning the resurrection of the dead, the hope of eternal life, and the kingdom of heaven, when they think their pages are full of falsehoods on facts which they themselves have learnt from experience and the light of reason? Reckless and incompetent expounders of holy Scripture bring untold trouble and sorrow on their wiser brethren when they are caught in one of their mischievous false opinions and are taken to task by those who are not bound by the authority of our sacred books. For then, to defend their utterly foolish and obviously untrue statements, they will try to call upon Holy Scripture for proof and even recite from memory many passages which they think support their position, although "they understand neither what they say nor the things about which they make assertion."[7]

In this passage St. Augustine seems to reject the idea of using Scripture to correct natural science. This is just a brief example of the type of writings that have transpired over the centuries regarding the validity of the Bible. This is not a new endeavor.

Augustine suggested two principles that relate to apparent conflicts between the Bible and secular knowledge, one indicating when secular knowledge claims should take priority and the other when a literal reading of the biblical text should prevail. The *principle of the priority of demonstration* suggested that if there is a conflict between a proven truth about nature and a particular reading of scripture, an alternative reading of Scripture must be sought. When an enquiry based on natural principles leads to a conclusion that appears to contradict scripture but cannot be doubted, then scripture must be reinterpreted. A second principle, the *principle of the priority of scripture* stated that when rational enquiry leads to something less than certainty, the authority of the literal sense of scripture is to be preferred. When there is an apparent conflict between a scripture passage and an assertion about the natural world grounded on sense or reason, the literal reading of the Scripture passage should prevail as long as the latter assertion lacks demonstration. These two ideas illustrate, to some extent, the written dialogue that existed regarding the apparent conflicts between scientific discoveries and the most accurate translations of the Bible, at the time. These principles are at least implicit in Augustine's *De Genesi ad litteram*, his commentary on the literal sense of Genesis and were accepted by medieval writers such as Thomas Aquinas. They were employed by the church authorities during the trial of Galileo, restated by Pope Leo XIII at the end of the nineteenth century, and invoked by Pope Pius XII in 1950 when condemning polygenism (the view that the human race had more than one origin).

Augustine further noted,

> In matters that are obscure and far beyond our vision, even in such as we may find treated in Holy Scripture, different interpretations are sometimes possible without prejudice to the faith we have received. In such a case, we should not rush in headlong and so firmly take our stand on one side that, if further progress in the search of truth justly undermines this position, we too fall with it. That would be to battle not for the teaching of Holy Scripture but for our own, wishing its teaching to conform to ours, whereas we ought to wish ours to conform to that of Sacred Scripture. This simply says that one should hold to it reasonably, and not unreasonably. But it is not reasonable to ignore reasonable arguments simply because they do not conclude with certainty.

Over the centuries, there has been apparent tension between

biblical criticism done by Catholics and non-Catholics alike. Such tension need not exist. Biblical study and an understanding of the material given to us by the Holy Spirit, over time, while true and communicative should eventually prove helpful to us all. Tension between bodies of the church over the Bible's authority only provided fuel for the secular world to remain skeptical of the Bible itself. A challenge of this book is to bring a perspective, not unknown to students of scripture over the centuries, that includes a demonstration of the Holy Spirit's work in the development of the Bible as it has been produced over the Millenia and as we have it affirmed in its present form today.

For many centuries therefore, debate and study of the Bible as authoritative has raged on as briefly suggested from some of the dialogue and writing, previously noted. Very devout students of scripture and very studious members of the scientific community have done their best to reconcile the two 'worlds' as it were. Rev John Wesley speaking in 1826 once said,

> Condemn no man for not thinking as you think. Let everyone enjoy the full and free liberty of thinking for himself. Let every man use his own judgment, since every man must give an account of himself to God. Abhor every approach, in any kind or degree, to the spirit of persecution, if you cannot reason nor persuade a man into the truth, never attempt to force a man into it. If love will not compel him to come, leave him to God, the judge of all.[8]

While many have sought to do this work of reconciliation between the Truth of the Bible and the recent developments of science, which has studied the world around us, one more voice might be helpful before we move on.

SPURGEON

Charles Hadden Spurgeon (1834-1892) a preacher in the 19th century has continued to be an impressive and faithful voice, through his writings, for the Truth of God's Word as we have it. He once said, "Visit many books but live in the Bible" or "Nobody ever outgrows Scripture; the book widens and deepens with our years."

In one of Spurgeon's sermons on the Bible, he stated as he briefly reviewed the various authors in answer to his question 'Who is the author?' "...each sentence was dictated by the Holy Spirit".[9] This claim was then and is now, an important consideration when thinking about the Bible. Later in his sermon he said: "First, my friends, stand over this volume, and *admire its authority*. This is no common book. It is not the sayings of the sages of Greece; here are not the utterances of philosophers of past ages. If these words were written by man, we might reject them; but O let me think the solemn thought, that this book is God's handwriting—that these words are God's!"[10] As Spurgeon raised the matter of 'authority' of the Bible, I as well raise it in this work. Hence the title, *By What Authority*.

BIBLICAL CRITICISM

There have also been over many years, and continue to be, verbal and written responses to the work of the German and British theologians who often appeared to be critical of the Scripture and its development over the last several centuries. To attempt to summarize the influence of biblical criticism over this period of time would be a monumental task. Re-reading some of the literature in this field and recalling studies from my seminary days has reminded me of the significant and excellent academic efforts that were developed to come to grips with some deeper understanding of the uniqueness of the Bible. There are several major types of biblical criticism that have challenged scholars and students of the Bible and continue to create dialogue about the work of the Holy Spirit in presenting scripture to all people.

Biblical criticism is an umbrella term for specific methods of studying the Bible. It is a discipline that studies textual, compositional and historical questions surrounding the Old and New Testaments. It lays the groundwork for meaningful interpretation of the Bible. Biblical criticism uses the grammar, structure, development, and relationship of language to identify such characteristics as the Bible's literary structure, its genre, its context, meaning, authorship and origins. It covers various techniques used mainly by mainline and liberal Christian theologians to study the meaning of Biblical passages. It uses general historical principles and is based primarily on reason rather than revelation or faith.

The historical-critical method of analyzing scripture ultimately questioned the reliability of the Bible. Biblical criticism originated with anti-Christian writers who valued reason and logic over faith and revelation. A goal was to discredit and ridicule the Bible and Christianity. Their analytical techniques were picked up by some liberal theologians and initially used to explain away and discount Biblical accounts of prophecy, miracles, or personal demon infestation.

Biblical criticism is a discipline that includes a wide range of approaches and questions within four major contemporary methodologies or types: textual, source, form, and literary criticism. Textual criticism examines the text and its manuscripts to identify what the original text would have said. Further, it is concerned with establishing the original or most authoritative text and also it involves philosophical influence which is the study of the biblical languages for an accurate knowledge of vocabulary, grammar and style of the period. Source criticism searches the texts for evidence of original sources. Form criticism identifies short units of text and seeks to identify their original setting. It classifies the written material according to the preliterary forms, such as parable or hymn. Each of these is primarily historical and pre-compositional in its concerns. Literary criticism, on the other hand, focuses on the literary structure, authorial purpose, and reader's response to the text through methods such as rhetorical criticism, canonical criticism, and narrative criticism. So it focuses on the various literary genres embedded in the text in order to uncover evidence concerning date of composition, authorship and original function of the various types of writing that constitute the Bible.

Biblical criticism lays a groundwork for meaningful interpretation of the Bible. Other schools of biblical criticism that are more exegetical in intent, that is more concerned with recovering original meanings of texts are: Redaction criticism which studies how the documents were assembled by their final authors and editors, and Historical criticism which seeks to interpret biblical writings in the context of their historical settings. Some prominent students of scripture within the Christian church have challenged Biblical criticism, as a field of science.

German pietism played a role in the development of Biblical criticism as did British deism, with its greatest influences being rationalism and protestant scholarship. German pietism was a religious reform movement that began among German Lutherans in the 17th century. It emphasized personal faith against the main Lutheran church's perceived stress on doctrine and theology over Christian living. Pietism quickly spread and later became concerned with social and educational matters. Pietism is a movement within Lutheranism that combines its emphasis on biblical doctrine with the Reformed emphasis on individual piety and living a vigorous Christian life. Although the movement initially was active exclusively within Lutheranism, it had a tremendous impact on Protestantism worldwide, particularly in North America and Europe.

British Deism, the religious attitude typical of the Enlightenment especially in France and England, holds that the only way the existence of God can be proven is to combine the application of reason with observation of the world. A Deist is one who believes in the existence of a God or Supreme being but denies revealed religion, basing their belief on the light of nature and reason. Deism was often synonymous with so-called natural religion because its principles are drawn from nature and human reasoning. In contrast to Deism there are many cultural religions or revealed religions, such as Judaism, Trinitarian Christianity, Islam, Buddhism, and others, which believe in supernatural intervention of God in the world; Deism denies any supernatural intervention.

In philosophy, rationalism is the epistemological (investigates origin, nature, methods and limits of human knowledge) view that regards reason as the chief source and test of knowledge or any view appealing to reason as a source of knowledge or justification. More formally, rationalism is defined as a methodology or a theory in which the criterion of the truth is not sensory but intellectual and deductive. So, in the late twentieth and early twenty-first century, Biblical criticism was influenced by a wide range of additional academic disciplines and theoretical perspectives changing it from a primarily historical approach to a multidisciplinary field.

As modernism spread through the succeeding decades, the tension between the influence of the sacred scriptures and the fields of biblical criticism increased. In my time of graduate studies at a secular university in the late 1960's the two seemed to be always at odds. Through the work of some German theologians, we find a continued effort to divide up the scriptures. Criticisms of the work of these theologians over the decades include the idea that many of them did not allow for the supernatural in their belief systems.

What conservative Biblical thinkers of that time seemed to oppose was the use of Biblical criticism by rationalists, thinkers of little faith or no faith at all. An eventual result of Biblical criticism was the inference that some of the Bible is the work of the Holy Spirit because it agrees with one's 'senses' and observations and some of the Bible cannot be true because it conflicts with current scientific theories, common practice or 'common sense'. Is it possible that 'common sense' is also influenced by external experience that varies due to one's ability to fully grasp the world around them? Addressing Moses, the Father through the Holy Spirit, commented in the midst of an extremely difficult time for Israel and his leadership of them:

> Remember how the Lord your God led you all the way in the wilderness these forty years, to humble and test you in order to know what was in your heart, whether or not you would keep his commands. He humbled you, causing you to hunger and then feeding you with manna, which neither you nor your ancestors had known, to teach you that man does not live on bread alone but on every word that comes from the mouth of the Lord. (Deuteronomy 8:2-3)

Possibly the Father has limited human ability to totally grasp the intricacies of Creation and one's total engagement with the world around them, including the development of the Bible.

In a field historically dominated by white male protestants, more recently non-white scholars, women and those from the Jewish and Catholic traditions have become prominent voices in Biblical criticism. Globalization brought a broader spectrum of worldviews into the field and other academic disciplines as diverse as Near Eastern studies, psychology, anthropology and sociology have formed new methods of biblical criticism such as socio-scientific criticism and psychological biblical criticism. Meanwhile post-modernism and post-critical interpretation began questioning biblical criticism's role and function.

Some of the written examples of discourse over the recent centuries illustrate the tension that existed and continues to exist between science and faith, between the Bible and secular discernment and "current" knowledge. The following material seeks to briefly illustrate the type of debating that has existed, both in dialogue and in written form, over several centuries that has addressed the apparent contradictions between reason and faith.

The scientific principles on which modern criticism is based depend in part upon viewing the Bible as a suitable object for literary study, rather than as an exclusively sacred text. Evaluation of the Scriptures to uncover evidence about historical matters was formerly called "higher criticism," a term first used with reference to writings of the German biblical scholar J.G. Eichhorn who applied the method to his study of the Pentateuch. In the 20th century, Rudolf Bultmann and Martin Dibelius initiated form criticism as a different approach to the study of historical circumstances surrounding biblical texts. The rapid development of philology (the study of literary texts, their form and meaning) in the 19th century together with archaeological discoveries of the 20th century revolutionized biblical criticism.

The concept of myth as a tool for interpreting the Bible was also introduced. This concept was picked up by Rudolf Bultmann and it became particularly influential in the early twentieth century. A typical written discourse during the German Enlightenment challenged the authorship of Genesis, known as textual criticism. There was a willingness among the doctoral candidates to re-express Christian doctrine in terms of the scientific method and the historical understanding common during the German enlightenment (circa 1750–1850).

A brief look at biblical criticism from the 17th through the 19th centuries suggests, amongst many other things, that a view of the Bible as inspired by the Holy Spirit in whole, not just in parts, has been severely challenged and damaged. As I have already noted, one of the basic or fundamental results of the proliferation of literature over those centuries by serious and intelligent writers is that the Bible came to be viewed as a series of writings some of which are inspired by Holy Spirit authorship and some which were not. The result has been that 'human' interpretation of the scriptures has become the determining factor as to which parts of the Bible were inspired and which were authored by human writers only: thus, up for challenge and critique. Over many centuries much has been written, debated and challenged regarding the truth of the Bible as we have it, under the influence of the Holy Spirit.

Biblical criticism then and now is not necessarily negative, in my view. It is research. It does not have a 'value' attached to it. It is a form of study. How we view the results of various forms of biblical criticism is personal and often determined by our faith stance. Biblical criticism began as an aspect of the rise of modern culture (modernity) in the West. Some scholars claim that its roots reach back to the Reformation but most agree it grew out of the German Enlightenment. The Enlightenment age and its skepticism of biblical and ecclesiastical authority ignited questions concerning the historical basis for the life of the man Jesus, which were dealt with separately from traditional theological views concerning Him. This 'quest' for the Jesus of history began in biblical criticism's earliest stages, reappeared in the nineteenth century and again in the twentieth, remaining a major occupation of biblical criticism, on and off, for over 200 years.

However, a result of such study over the recent centuries has had an effect of undermining confidence in the God's Word, to all people. It has influenced many to take apart the verses or texts of scripture, piece by piece, seeking to determine whether some verses were spoken to humankind by the Holy Spirit and thus were 'Truth' and some were not spoken by the Holy Spirit but were influenced by one's current understanding of the universe or morality and therefore not considered as part of the 'inspired' document given to humankind. A problem with this development, over the centuries, is that these are decisions of individual students with their limited understanding of the world and creation, who have determined which verses are "Inspired" and which verses could not have been authored by the Holy Spirit. This approach has allowed for individual students of scripture and commentators, in their considered opinion, to 'decide for themselves', based on a particular personal 'history', which texts influence their theological views and which contradict with their views and therefore were not 'inspired by the Holy Spirit'

The continuous debate regarding the authority of the Scriptures and its origin has not lessened in our day. The Church of today continues to wrestle with the apparent contradictions between the 'truth' of the Scriptures and the practices of parishioners and the non-churched alike, as they daily live out their lives within all present cultures, worldwide. This debate is not new. It is not addressed here for the first time but I feel it needs, in our day and age, to be addressed by and to the Church, once again.

Endnotes

1. Dale Kuiper, "The Bible, a Divine Book: John Calvin's Doctrine of Holy Scripture" in *The Standard Bearer*. (Jenison, MI: Reformed Free Publishing Association, 1993) Vol 2.
2. Kuiper, *The Bible*, 85.
3. Kuiper, *The Bible*, 103.
4. Kuiper, T*he Bible*, 103.
5. Kuiper, *The Bible*, 106.
6. Kuiper, *The Bible*, 108.
7. St. Augustine, *The Literal Meaning of Genesis* (www.ancient.eu/article/91), Vol. 2, 2012.
8. John Wesley, *The Works of the Rev. John Wesley* (London: Printed at the Conference office, 1809), 421.
9. Charles Haddon Spurgeon, *Sermons of Rev. C.H. Spurgeon of London*, Vol 1, Sermon II, (New York: Funk & Wagnalls, 1857), 23-44].
10. Spurgeon, Sermons, 29-30.

Chapter 4

A BRIEF HISTORY OF BIBLICAL INSPIRATION

Throughout the history of Christian thought debate has therefore raged regarding the authority of the Bible's claims, statements, and pronouncements regarding religious practice and relevance.

Verses have been challenged and contextualization has been involved in attempting to understand the words of Holy Scripture, the stories, the miracles recorded and historical connections discovered. Archeology continues to this day to bring relevance, through newly discovered artifacts and unearthed objects, to the truth of the historical accuracy of the Bible. Nevertheless, the Bible has never been understood as being written for the purpose of historical proof or geographical accuracy. Part of my theological education and that of all Christian pastors includes the study of the relevant debates on Inspiration, many of which took place in the 19th century, but also from earliest times. Deism rejected the inspiration of Scripture.

Biblical inspiration is the doctrine in Christian theology which suggests that the authors and editors of the Bible were led or influenced by God with the result that their writings may be designated in some sense the very Word of God. I will move this argument along to suggest and demonstrate that this work accomplished by the Father, to bring about this truth, was done through the deliberate action of the Holy Spirit, the third person of the Trinity. The Holy

Spirit influenced men and women to experience, to remember and to write, their encounters with the Holy. "For prophecy never had its origin in the human will, but prophets, though human, spoke from God as they were carried along by the Holy Spirit" (2 Peter 1:21). This argument will be supported further in our chapter on the role of prophecy in scripture.

The influence of the Holy Spirit on the Church has not ceased to this day. Even before the Church was established as recorded in Acts, Jesus promised believers that they would experience the support of the Holy Spirit: "Whenever you are arrested and brought to trial, do not worry beforehand about what to say. Just say whatever is given you at the time, for it is not you speaking, but the Holy Spirit" (Mark 13:11), and (Luke 12:12). Also, "But the Advocate, the Holy Spirit, whom the Father will send in my name, will teach you all things and will remind you of everything I have said to you" (John 14:26). and, "We are witnesses of these things, and so is the Holy Spirit, whom God has given to those who obey him" (Acts 5:32).

Further the doctrine of Inerrancy which refers to the fact that the Bible was without error when it was created (heard and later written) pushed the idea of Divine influence in the development of the Word to all people, over the millennia. In spite of the suggestions of apparent contradictions within the Bible, created in part by the work of German and British biblical criticism, influence by the Holy Spirit continues today, through the preached word, through ongoing miracles and the ultimate miracle of personal salvation through Jesus Christ.

"And hope does not put us to shame, because God's love has been poured out into our hearts through the Holy Spirit, who has been given to us" (Romans 5:5). or "And you also were included in Christ when you heard the message of truth, the gospel of your salvation. When you believed, you were marked in him with a seal, the promised Holy Spirit, who is a deposit guaranteeing our inheritance until the redemption of those who are God's possession—to the praise of his glory" (Ephesians 1:13-14). and "Guard the good deposit that was entrusted to you—guard it with the help of the Holy Spirit who lives in us" (2 Tim 1:14).

Classic to the believer's view of faith is an understanding of Inspiration that prompted the writings of the Bible. For the purposes of this book the word 'believer' means one who has professed faith in Jesus Christ as Lord and Saviour at some time in their life, by experience, at an age of understanding. Follow-up in that experience includes believers' baptism, a sense of the Mission given by the Father to all people and commitment to the local church. The use of the term 'believer' as I am using it and understood in recent times comes, in part, from a national-wide study accomplished by churches in Canada in May of 1973 sponsored by Canadian Baptists and Mennonites.

The individual who is a believer is therefore old enough to come to an understanding of who Jesus is through the Biblical revelation as we have it, written from past millennia. In the early 1970's I recall a meeting of believers in Canada, in Winnipeg. The intent of the gathering was to come to an agreement amongst themselves to a current definition of the "Believers' Church". The recent origin of the 'Believers Church' comes from the first convention which met in 1967 at the Southern Baptist Theological Seminary. Those gathered later, in Winnipeg, included Pentecostals, Baptists, Mennonites, Alliance and other believing groups who desired to give a definition to a 'believer' as understood from the Bible. A refreshing of this definition was critical at the time, in my view. It juxtaposed this definition against centuries of confusion about who the Church is. Historical documentary about the rise and fall of so many 'Christian' groups and sects had brought confusion to our Western culture and even world culture. What is a Christian? Who is 'in' and who is 'out'? Unfortunately, I am not yet convinced that that event in 1973 solved all of the dichotomy and the debate amongst people of faith but it contributed significantly to my understanding of the concept, which continued to influence my pastoral ministry. While my experience of the term 'believers' church' was helpful at the time, obviously a similar term was used earlier in many contexts, by those referring to Christians.

The Bible as we have it today has been given by the Father to all of humanity, all of us. A friend used an acrostic to explain the importance of the BIBLE: "**B**asic **I**nstructions **B**efore **L**eaving **E**arth". A response of faith to what the Bible says about sin, loss, and failure, which are common to us all, and further what the Bible states of the truth and affirmation regarding forgiveness, confession and assurance, brings one to become a 'believer'. The historical definitions of church as a building or a denomination mean little to this definition of a believer. All who have made a profession of faith in Jesus Christ and have publicly confirmed that act are believers, the Church, and will join together in heaven, for eternity. (Appendix A).

Interestingly, belief in the inspiration of scripture comes from the Scripture itself. The Holy Spirit inspired Timothy to write, several decades after Jesus' death and resurrection,

> And how from infancy you have known the Holy Scriptures, which are able to make you wise for salvation through faith in Christ Jesus. All Scripture is God-breathed and is useful for teaching, rebuking, correcting and training in righteousness, so that the servant of God may be thoroughly equipped for every good work." (2 Timothy 3:15-17)

'God breathed' has been considered, for centuries, the Greek term for 'inspiration'. The Father through the work of His Holy Spirit, the third person of the Trinity, moved men and women to speak the 'words of the Father' to humanity through spoken and eventual written communication. To this young pastor, Paul wrote that all scripture is inspired by the Father through the work of the Holy Spirit. This would include the scriptures of the Old Testament, familiar to Paul and to Timothy, as well. Also understood is that Paul, through that same Holy Spirit, included the scriptures of the New Testament, later confirmed by the several church Councils of the 3rd century. Such has been the simple understanding of 'inspiration' for centuries.

A BRIEF HISTORY OF BIBLICAL INSPIRATION

The believer's understanding of scripture is that the authority and inspiration of the Bible is accomplished by the initial and ongoing influence of the Holy Spirit from the beginning of its creation, to the present. The writing done through human thought and experience was always done under the direction of the Holy Spirit. The Holy Spirit used the effective tool of prophecy to bring about predictions of future events that have since occurred and have been affirmed by writers who also made prophetic contributions, centuries later. The Holy Spirit continues to influence the understanding and influence of the scriptures.

An illustration is offered to us in the following writing from the apostle Peter to the church, at that time. The authority comes from the clear and affirmed presence of prophecy. The definition of prophecy, the definition of a prophet and the ongoing support of the Holy Spirit contribute to this understanding of the authority of the Bible, for current believers. Peter wrote,

> We also have the prophetic message as something completely reliable, and you will do well to pay attention to it, as to a light shining in a dark place, until the day dawns and the morning star rises in your hearts. Above all, you must understand that no prophecy of Scripture came about by the prophet's own interpretation of things. For prophecy never had its origin in the human will, but prophets, though human, spoke from God as they were carried along by the Holy Spirit." (2 Peter 1:19-21)

Peter, also a follower and disciple of Jesus, reminded his readers again only decades after Jesus' resurrection, "So I will always remind you of these things, even though you know them and are firmly established in the truth you now have. I think it is right to refresh your memory as long as I live in the tent of this body, because I know that I will soon put it aside, as our Lord Jesus Christ has made clear to me. And I will make every effort to see that after my departure you will always be able to remember these things" (2 Peter 1:12-15). Throughout history, from time to time, followers of Jesus need to be reminded of the truths of God's plan to rescue all people, for an eternity with Him. Hence this book.

This material presented here has been referred to and believed by biblical scholars and writers over many centuries, as you will note in following chapters. However, I believe the time is right to remind the Church of these truths once again. Developments in the West have convinced me that an understanding of the significance of the Holy's Spirit's work on behalf of the Bible is critical to our day. The Bible has often been ridiculed. This is not new, of course. It has been critically torn apart enough for the suggestion to be made that some passages are the work of the Holy Spirit in origin and some are not the work of the Holy Spirit. There are some reasons in biblical history why that has occurred. The apparent unequal weight currently placed on all sacred texts, from all of the faith traditions, has seemed more prominent in my lifetime bringing about a frustration of immense proportion. Over recent years the various 'news cycles' on this subject, that have caught my attention, indicate a significant lack of knowledge regarding 'competing' interpretations and views of the religions of the world.

I recall my experience with an introduction to an anthropology course in the early 1960's. My experience is much 'dated' but nevertheless relevant to this book. From that Introduction came an understanding that according to this new science of anthropology, all religious material fits a category of myths, etc. I learned that anthropological studies of religion constituted some of the most important thinking at the time in the development of religious studies, as a field. To some extent, it was suggested that all major theories of religious evolution can be considered "anthropological" because they all in some way seek to compare and understand "religious" phenomena of various cultures across the world, over time. The anthropology of religion has often centered on those sociocultural elements that are frequently identified as religious: myths, rituals, magic, beliefs about gods and divine beings, taboos, and symbols. To assist us in attempting to clarify the importance of an understanding that the

Christian faith is not one of those 'world religions', as propositioned in the science of anthropology, consider an illustration.

When I was young my cousin, who is my age, and I used to argue about cars. His dad drove a Chev and my dad drove a Ford. So, often we would compare and each suggest that one car was better than the other. It was a 'family' thing. We carried that rivalry for some years. After high school he and I went our separate ways. Decades later, we met at the occasion of a memorial service and I noticed he was driving a Ford! At that time, I was driving a Chev. The significance of our youthful debates was clear to me as I reflected, various car models do not matter, in the end. At All. They all get one from A to B and hopefully back to A.

So it is with all world religions, based on the definitions provided in the science of anthropology. They are important to study, to understand people groups, their history and development of a group's religious belief often, if not always, obtained from family experience and teaching. But they are all the same, one is as important as the other. They were often developed and are currently promoted by sincere seekers, who study this world in which humans have existed and do exist.

However, the Christian faith is not a religion, it is a relationship. As we will further discover, the method and means that God the Father has communicated and is communicating his love and care for humanity came from Him, not from people seeking to discover Him or from their experiences. Paul wrote,

> But God demonstrates his own love for us in this: While we were still sinners, Christ died for us. Since we have now been justified by his blood, how much more shall we be saved from God's wrath through him! For if, while we were God's enemies, we were reconciled to him through the death of his Son, how much more, having been reconciled, shall we be saved through his life! Not only is this so, but we also boast in God through our Lord Jesus Christ, through whom we have now received reconciliation. (Romans 5:8-11)

God first sought out all humanity, continues to do so, clarifies our fallenness, our separation from Him and provides a means to reconciliation with Himself. "For the Lord is the great God, the great King above all gods" (Psalm 95:3).

My early reflection and study of this anthropological material was later challenged by my studies at Seminary, as I came to understand the significance of the work of the Holy Spirit in particular and singularly on the development, over the many millennia, of the Bible as we have it. I discovered afresh the uniqueness of this Work in the context of many ancient texts and oral statements that continue to make up the beliefs of the religions of the world. As far as this book is concerned these biblical texts referred to above, tie the work of the Holy Spirit throughout the development of the current scriptures with those who put the writings together, who related their experiences of the Father and their environment to the 'message' for Israel and for the Church. Israel was taken under the Father's 'wing', chosen as God's people in the context of a lost world, to tell that world Who God is. However, the Father knew the Church would be created eventually. From the beginning of the challenge to Israel, there was a presumed and expected failure of Israel's spiritual leadership, over centuries, to effectively 'tell the world Who God is' as they were commanded to do.

In Exodus 6:7-8 we read,

> I will take you as my own people, and I will be your God. Then you will know that I am the Lord your God, who brought you out from under the yoke of the Egyptians. And I will bring you to the land I swore with uplifted hand to give to Abraham, to Isaac and to Jacob. I will give it to you as a possession. I am the Lord.

And, "From the rocky peaks I see them, from the heights I view them. I see a people who live apart and do not consider themselves one of the nations" (Numbers 23:9). Further, "For the LORD has chosen Jacob to be his own, Israel to be his treasured possession" (Psalm

135:4). "But now, this is what the LORD says - he who created you, Jacob, he who formed you, Israel: "Do not fear, for I have redeemed you; I have summoned you by name; you are mine" (Isaiah 43:1).

And finally,

> I will go before you and will level the mountains; I will break down gates of bronze and cut through bars of iron. I will give you hidden treasures, riches stored in secret places, so that you may know that I am the LORD, the God of Israel, who summons you by name. For the sake of Jacob my servant, of Israel my chosen, I summon you by name and bestow on you a title of honor, though you do not acknowledge me. I am the LORD, and there is no other; apart from me there is no God. I will strengthen you, though you have not acknowledged me, so that from the rising of the sun to the place of its setting people may know there is none besides me. I am the LORD, and there is no other." (Isaiah 45:2-6)

Much of the Old Testament describes the unique relationship between God the Father and Israel. They were chosen to communicate an understanding of the Creator God and His call for all peoples to acknowledge His love for them. This mandate gives humanity a reason for living, an identity that supersedes all other identities that the 'world' chases. However, later in the Old Testament, understood through the writing of the prophets in particular, it is to be noted that the priesthood also failed to follow the call to faithfulness to the Father that His message had challenged. God was and is not pleased with Israel, with her communication to the peoples of the world. Isaiah 5 describes the disappointment of the Father towards Israel's behaviour.

It is a picture of a vineyard given to His beloved, prepared by the Father and blessed with all goodness. Isaiah 5:7 states, "The vineyard of the LORD Almighty is the nation of Israel, and the people of Judah are the vines he delighted in. And he looked for justice, but saw bloodshed; for righteousness, but heard cries of distress." Over the centuries, Israel has become such that "when I looked for good grapes, why did it yield only bad?" (Isaiah 5:4b) This theme is very prevalent in the Old Testament scriptures, as the Holy Spirit communicates through the prophets what has been the result of generations of unfaithfulness and failure to communicate the nature and love of the Father, to all the nations. "I had planted you like a choice vine of sound and reliable stock. How then did you turn against me into a corrupt, wild vine?" (Jeremiah 2:21) Ezekiel referred o Jerusalem, a main city in Israel, as a useless vine. (Ezekiel 15). Ezekiel and Isaiah describe the eventual 'captivity' due to unfaithfulness. "Israel was a spreading vine; he brought forth fruit for himself. As his fruit increased, he built more altars; as his land prospered, he adorned his sacred stones. Their heart is deceitful, and now they must bear their guilt. The LORD will demolish their altars and destroy their sacred stones" (Hosea 10:1-2).

The challenge placed upon Israel to 'tell the world Who God is' was eventually, over many generations, ignored and failed to communicate this message to other peoples. Hence the Church was established in the New Testament record as Christ, God Himself in the flesh, came to bring a challenge to the nations: God loves us, created us, forgave us on the Cross and longs to have an eternal relationship with each of us. The Inspired scriptures, from the beginning of written and recorded history, continued to communicate to the nations of the world 'Who God is'.

In Psalm 80, the writer recognizes that the Lord has abandoned Israel. Throughout the Old Testament, the cry of some is given, "Restore us, God Almighty; make your face shine on us, that we may be saved" (Psalms 80:7). The task had failed and all the nations yet did not know God, the God of Israel. The challenge continues, by God's grace. The Father even chose a Pharaoh to do the task: "For Scripture says to Pharaoh, 'I raised you up for this very purpose, that I might display my power in you and that my name might be proclaimed in all the earth'" (Romans 9:17). I am not suggesting, further, that the Church has completely succeeded in the challenge, either. Far from that.

Further in Romans,[1]

> One of you will say to me: "Then why does God still blame us? For who is able to resist his will?" But who are you, a human being, to talk back to God? "Shall what is formed say to the one who formed it, 'Why did you make me like this?'" Does not the potter have the right to make out of the same lump of clay some pottery for special purposes and some for common use? What if God, although choosing to show his wrath and make his power known, bore with great patience the objects of his wrath-prepared for destruction? What if he did this to make the riches of his glory known to the objects of his mercy, whom he prepared in advance for glory-even us, whom he also called, not only from the Jews but also from the Gentiles? As he says in Hosea: "I will call them 'my people' who are not my people; and I will call her 'my loved one' who is not my loved one," and, "In the very place where it was said to them, 'You are not my people,' there they will be called 'children of the living God.'" Isaiah cries out concerning Israel: "Though the number of the Israelites be like the sand by the sea, only the remnant will be saved. For the LORD will carry out his sentence on earth with speed and finality." It is just as Isaiah said previously: "Unless the LORD Almighty had left us descendants, we would have become like Sodom, we would have been like Gomorrah." What then shall we say? That the Gentiles, who did not pursue righteousness, have obtained it, a righteousness that is by faith; but the people of Israel, who pursued the law as the way of righteousness, have not attained their goal. Why not? Because they pursued it not by faith but as if it were by works. They stumbled over the stumbling stone. As it is written: "See, I lay in Zion a stone that causes people to stumble and a rock that makes them fall, and the one who believes in him will never be put to shame." (Romans 9:19-33)

Paul's reference here is to Jesus Christ. The Father never abandoned Israel when the task of proclaiming 'Who God is' had failed but made a Way possible for all humankind to find redemption, through the finished work of Christ on the Cross. For Israel, and everyone else, a new plan of human redemption and reconciliation was to be set up, understood as having needed to be activated from the beginning of 'time'. It is still in effect according to the inspired Word of God, the Bible, even though Israel, being human, was expected by the Father to fail to deliver. From the very beginning of Creation, it is understood that it would be the Church which was going to be established, through the finished work of Jesus Christ on the Cross, to continue the task of rescuing humanity for the rest of time.

Following chapters will introduce the purpose of prophecy and the work of prophets throughout biblical history, in bringing us an 'authentic' Word from God, for all people. The Bible is the only 'work' for humankind and I will endeavour to substantiate this concept. Second Peter 1:19-21 is a key theme of this book. As a result of a weak view of biblical inspiration, over many centuries, it has been suggested that some biblical texts are not 'inspired' but are added by the writer without the 'signature' of the Holy Spirit. Hence the end result has been that individual theologians, teachers and students of scripture have made their own critique of various parts of the Bible. Those verses of a particular passage, with which one does not agree, are therefore critiqued as not 'inspired' by the Holy Spirit and thus not part of the Word of God to the Church, according to this developed theology. Inspiration, the work of the Holy Spirit, ties the whole of the Bible together whether or not we understand all of it, at any current moment in human history.

Endnotes

1   Dale Moody, *Romans*, in The Broadman Bible Commentary, ed. Clifton J. Allen (Nashville, Broadman Press, 1971), Vol 10:231-233.

BY WHAT AUTHORITY

Chapter 5

JESUS' VIEW OF THE SCRIPTURES

One of the most fascinating studies involves the discovery of Jesus' view of the same scriptures that the Church trusts today. Obviously, He would have referred to the Old Testament in His familiarity of the Bible at that time so we must also look at some of that material in our consideration of an inspired Bible. The Christian faith includes a simple understanding of the significance of Jesus of Nazareth, His birth, life, death and resurrection. What Jesus taught has influenced the Church for nearly 2 millennia, long before most other religious leaders were born or influenced a faithful following. What Jesus thought of the Hebrew writings is critical to the discussion of this book. The suggestion that these spoken words, later written down by inspired scribes, are of such significant import to an understanding of the whole of the Bible today, begs the question as to what Jesus' view of them might be. How important is the Bible anyway in the light of so many other writings of religion that are at our fingertips today, writings that have influenced and continue to influence millions of the worlds' peoples? Jesus' view matters.

One of many ways to understand what Jesus thought of *God's Word*, which was communicated to the Hebrew tribe and eventually to us all, is to look briefly at one of His parables found in Luke 8. It is the parable of the seeds. Jesus stated that the seed is the word of

God (Luke 8:11). "Whoever has ears to hear, let them hear" (Luke 8:8). The **word** of God is like a **seed** in the context of all that can happen to it, once it is released. Once released, responses vary. One response is noted when the devil takes that word from their hearts, so they eventually do not believe the word which was sown. Another response is a loss that eventually occurs for those, represented by rocky ground, who believe the word for a while until they are tested. They hear the word but have no root and the testing of life kills their belief. The seed that fell amongst thorns refers to those who hear the word, the seed that was spread. Life's worries, riches and pleasures choke the word from their hearts and they eventually fail to believe. Then lastly, those who had a noble and good heart hear the word and retain it for life.

For Jesus the hearing, understanding and taking in of God's Word meant life, meant making a difference in all relationships. The scriptures for Jesus are authentic and life changing. Jesus used scripture in His teaching when he traveled in ministry. "Not until halfway through the festival did Jesus go up to the temple courts and begin to teach. The Jews there were amazed and asked, 'How did this man get such learning without having been taught?' Jesus answered, 'My teaching is not my own. It comes from the one who sent me'" (John 7:14-16).

He believed every word of scripture. It was written by the Holy Spirit's inspiration even though the pen was held by people. He still quoted it as God's authority. For example, Jesus quoted from Genesis 2:24, "'Haven't you read,' he replied, 'that at the beginning the Creator made them male and female, and said, 'For this reason a man will leave his father and mother and be united to his wife, and the two will become one flesh'? So they are no longer two, but one flesh. Therefore what God has joined together, let no one separate" (Matthew 19:4-5).

He was answering the Pharisees' question: "Is it lawful for a man to divorce his wife for any and every reason?" (Matthew 19:3).

The discussion continued between Jesus and his disciples which is interesting in this day to consider, as well. Put simply, Jesus used the Holy Spirit inspired book of Genesis to confront the thinking of the day. He believed it was relevant to the discussion, brought about by inquiry into very important concepts. The same applies today. That same Old Testament inspired by the same Holy Spirit continues to have application to our world and our relationships. Jesus used the material from the Old Testament and therefore Scripture should be used in current consideration of relevant topics in our culture. The Bible is the plumb line which measures the cultures of the day, here in the Western world or in the Eastern countries.

Jesus believed Abel was a real individual, as he spoke harshly against Israel (Luke 11:51) and He believed in Abraham (John 8:56-58). He also believed the scriptures about Noah.

> As it was in the days of Noah, so it will be at the coming of the Son of Man. For in the days before the flood, people were eating and drinking, marrying and giving in marriage, up to the day Noah entered the ark; and they knew nothing about what would happen until the flood came and took them all away. That is how it will be at the coming of the Son of Man." (Matthew 24:37-39)

He tied in the experienced truth about the flood and the coming of the Son of Man. Both events are true and happened, according to the Bible; Jesus believed in their reality, in the truth of the Old Testament writings.

All the prophecies of the Old Testament regarding Jesus were fulfilled. Jesus was familiar with and believed in the Old Testament references to Himself and that they would be fulfilled while He was on this earth. He knew of and believed in the words of Isaiah 53 which refers to the 4th servant (the suffering servant), distinct from the servant Israel.[1] **(See Isaiah 53:1-12)**.

This "servant song" has been called 'the most influential poem of any literature', the highest peak of Old Testament revelation' and the 'heart of the Old Testament'. Jesus knew this prophecy. The writers of the New Testament quoted this chapter often and almost all of it is located in their writings, produced centuries later. This servant song is definitely about an individual and not a nation. (Isaiah 53:8-9) The Exile of Israel was a punishment for a nation, as the prophet stated elsewhere, but this text is about one person. Jesus knew this, as well. He knew the text of Isaiah 53 was referring to an act completed, a triumph over suffering. References to his suffering were in the past tense, "He was despised and rejected" (53:3); "he was wounded for our transgressions" (53:5); he was cut off from the land of the living" (53:8). On the other hand the verbs that speak of his triumph and glory are to be translated in the future tense: "See, my servant will act wisely" (52:13); he shall see his offspring, he shall prolong his days" (53:10); he shall divide the spoil with the strong (53:12). Some sufferers are saviours. Jesus knew this as He came amongst us and lived a life prepared for the Cross, for suffering and pain (53:3). He took up the plan of the Father willingly for our salvation and eternal healing. (53:4-5) Jesus knew this scripture and lived amongst us, on this earth, nonetheless.

Another of the ways to obtain Jesus' view of the scripture is to research the Bible for some of the many other incidents to which He referred. There are many references of Jesus referring to oral and later written scriptures from centuries earlier, which were then applied to Himself at the time of his life on this earth. Again, the Holy Spirit is influencing this relationship and dependence. The Holy Spirit has not taken His influence away from these interactions, the results of which we can obtain and understand even centuries later.

In Matthew 21:23 and following, we read that as Jesus came to Jerusalem he was confronted by the religious leadership of the Hebrew faith. His practice of teaching was often challenged by those who heard him speak. "By what authority are you doing these things? Who gave you this authority?" They did recognize he had authority but the source of it was of a consternation to them. After a response with a trick question to these leaders, Jesus answered: "Neither will I tell you **by what authority** I am doing these things" (Matthew 21:27). That is the question of some of the leadership who encountered Jesus. Jesus was aware that His authority came from the Father, from the dawn of creation. That is the question that needs to be put to any religious leaders or spiritual prognosticators that come across our path. By what authority do you present your claims? Whether you be prophet or angel? That is the question we each need to ask for ourselves. The answer can influence our eternal security, in Heaven.

Jesus' view of the scriptures is noticed later in Mathew 21:42. Knowing these same leaders were listening, Jesus asked while talking about who may enter the Kingdom of God, "Have you never read the scriptures: the stone the builders rejected has become the cornerstone; the Lord has done this, and it is marvelous in our eyes". (Psalm 118:22-23) He knew he was that 'stone'. Jesus had a strong view of the Old Testament scripture. Almost as an aside while in discussion with some Jewish opponents of Him, Jesus stated, "**and Scripture cannot be set aside**" (John 10:35b).

Further to Jesus' view of scripture, in Matthew 26:54 he stated during his arrest, "But how then would the Scriptures be fulfilled that say it must happen in this way?" The Old Testament had already prophesied how Jesus would die. (Isaiah 53:7-11) That death on a cross would again support the validity of the scriptures of which Jesus completely believed and then saw fulfilled. In this text, Matthew 26:53-4, the suggestion of twelve legions of angels saving him, which was a possibility, would not fulfill the prophecy. Jesus viewed the scripture to be prophetic, authoritative and completely accurate for his life, death and resurrection. Again, with reference Jesus' arrest, Mark quoted Jesus as saying of his life on the earth, "But the scriptures must be fulfilled" (Mark 14:49).

In the context of Luke 4:18-19 Jesus was in the synagogue, the Hebrew place of worship. On the Sabbath, the holy day, He was handed a passage of scripture to read. It was taken from the prophet Isaiah, written centuries earlier and significant to the hearers there.

"The Spirit of the LORD is on me, because he has anointed me to proclaim good news to the poor. He has sent me to proclaim freedom for the prisoners and recovery of sight for the blind, to set the oppressed free, to proclaim the year of the LORD's favor" (Luke

4:18-19). It referred to an oracle of Isaiah which announced that he, Jesus, was divinely appointed to his task and endowed with the Spirit of the Lord. He was sent to proclaim a message that will affect a wonderous change to his discouraged listeners.[2] Jesus' view of the Holy Spirit's work, providing listeners with a thorough word from the Father, allowed him to take the initiative and proclaim that the prophet who spoke and wrote in the 8th century BC was making a future reference to the work of Jesus, Himself. The prophet gave an apt future portrayal of Jesus' own work, which would eventually come and which was then going on in that present time. That work would turn out to be his death on the Cross and his resurrection. He said, "Today this scripture is fulfilled in your hearing" (Luke 4:21). Jesus believed in the authority, the truth and the inclusive meaning of the scripture, for all.

Again, Jesus said, "You study the Scriptures diligently because you think that in them you have eternal life. These are the very scriptures that testify about me, yet you refuse to come to me to have life" (John 5:39-40). His belief about the scriptures being inspired by the Holy Spirit and thus Truth, influenced his rendering of his ministry, life, death and eventual resurrection. So, one might consider coming to Him, even today, to have life eternal.

A group of Sadducees, religious leaders of the day, challenged Jesus over the subject of the resurrection, about which they did not believe, even though resurrection is clearly mentioned in the 'inspired' Old Testament. Jesus said: "you are in error because you do not know the scriptures or the power of God" (Matthew 22:29). (See Matthew 22:23-32. See also Mark12:24-27 and the full story as well in Luke: 20:27-38). Jesus' view of scripture was that the religious leaders should know the Old Testament and believe in its inspiration, as He did. They should have known what Moses spoke and wrote regarding marriage and other accounts of resurrection or of life after this life. (See Enoch for example, Genesis 5:24 and Hebrews 11:5 or of Elijah. 2 Kings 2:10-11) They experienced the next life without experiencing death. This teaching by Jesus astonished (Matthew 22:33) those listening, even though they would have been less likely than the Sadducees to have known the Old Testament.

In Luke 24:27 Jesus "explained all that was said in the scriptures about himself" to the two he met on the road to Emmaus after His resurrection. He was responding to their queries as they walked along the road to their home. Queries about this Jesus of Nazareth who they knew and was killed on a cross. Then they had heard further of some angelic vision indicating this Jesus was alive, resurrected.

He had said to them, "How foolish you are, and how slow to believe all that the prophets have spoken! Did not the Messiah have to suffer these things and then enter his glory?" Jesus was fully in compliance regarding all that had been spoken of by the prophets and later written about the coming of the Messiah. Centuries had passed since these events were prophesied. In this text all was coming to pass that was written about in the Old Testament; writings about which these two, that he met, would have had the opportunity to become familiar.

After the resurrection, according to Luke, Jesus met his disciples. He again affirmed his view of the scriptures, written centuries earlier. He said to them,

> This is what I told you while I was still with you, "Everything must be fulfilled that is written about me in the Law of Moses, the Prophets and the Psalms." Then he opened their minds so they could understand the Scriptures. He told them, "This is what is written: The Messiah will suffer and rise from the dead on the third day, and repentance for the forgiveness of sins will be preached in his name to all nations, beginning at Jerusalem. You are witnesses of these things." (Luke 24:44-48)

There continues to be some debate about the fact that although Jesus believed the scriptures as they applied to Himself and referred to them in these several situations after His resurrection, it was really only after His Resurrection appearances to hundreds of witnesses that the fledging Church began to more fully come to understand the Old Testament references that applied to this Jesus. These same events were often misunderstood by Hebrew scholars of the time. Nevertheless, the Church was established on the truth of these events.

So today, the Church is mandated to continue this challenge that Jesus made to his followers. Preach this historic act of providing forgiveness for all people, all nations, which was set in prophetic words, inspired by the Holy Spirit who was then active in these events at the time of the crucifixion, death and resurrection of this Jesus of Nazareth, this Christ, Son of God and God Himself.

As Louis Gaussen had asserted,

> We are not afraid to say it: when we hear the Son of God quote the Scriptures, everything is said, in our view, on their divine inspiration—we need no further testimony. All the declarations of the Bible are, no doubt, equally divine; but this example of the Savior of the world has settled the question for us at once. This proof requires neither long nor learned researches; it is grasped by the hand of a child as powerfully as by that of a doctor. Should any doubt, then, assail your soul let it behold Him in the presence of the Scriptures![3]

When people today do not pay attention to the Scriptures, Jesus through those same inspired scriptures gives comment: "You are in error because you do not know the Scriptures or the power of God", (Matthew 22:29) or as Jesus replied in Mark 12:24, "Are you not in error because you do not know the Scriptures or the power of God?" Jesus knew the scriptures and believed in all of them, in the Old Testament and in the later fully inspired New Testament. The Holy Spirit was active in the final compilation of these sacred texts in the 3rd century, no less so than throughout the history of its compilation.

This understanding leads to the consideration that Jesus was subject to the Scriptures, concerning Himself.

Endnotes

1. Page H. Kelly, *Isaiah*, in The Broadman Bible Commentary, ed. Clifton J. Allen (Nashville, Broadman Press, 1971), Vol 5:340-345.
2. Kelly, *Isaiah*, 361-362.
3. Louis Gaussen, *The Divine Inspiration of Scripture* (Christian Focus Publications, 2007).

BY WHAT AUTHORITY

Chapter 6

JESUS WAS (is) SUBJECT TO SCRIPTURE

There are many instances in the New Testament where Jesus was subject to prophetic words from the Old Testament. A very unique experience that supports this truth was the experience with three of His disciples, Peter, James and John, on what became known as the Mount of Transfiguration where He was transfigured with Elijah and Moses,

> After six days Jesus took Peter, James and John with him and led them up a high mountain, where they were all alone. There he was transfigured before them. His clothes became dazzling white, whiter than anyone in the world could bleach them. And there appeared before them Elijah and Moses, who were talking with Jesus. Peter said to Jesus, "Rabbi, it is good for us to be here. Let us put up three shelters-one for you, one for Moses and one for Elijah." (He did not know what to say, they were so frightened.) Then a cloud appeared and covered them, and a voice came from the cloud: "This is my Son, whom I love. Listen to him!" Suddenly, when they looked around, they no longer saw anyone with them except Jesus. As they were coming down the mountain, Jesus gave them orders not to tell anyone what they had seen until the Son of Man had risen from the dead. They kept the matter to themselves, discussing what "rising from the dead" meant. (Mark 9:2-10)

All three Gospels refer to this experience after which Jesus asked them not to tell anyone what they witnessed until after His Resurrection. Whatever Jesus and two Old Testament prophets discussed that day, the experience certainly gave Jesus a 'heads up' to His future on this earth, in the coming few short years. He was playing a role that was predetermined.

According to this story the disciples, of course, questioned Jesus after the experience on the Mount of Transfiguration. They inquired of Him regarding Elijah, since he was there and seen, what was meant by references to the 'placement' of a returned Elijah in the prophetic message of the Old Testament. To this inquiry Jesus replied, "To be sure, Elijah does come first, and restores all things. Why then is it written that the Son of Man must suffer much and be rejected? But I tell you, Elijah has come, and they have done to him everything they wished, just as it is written about him" (Mark 9:12-13). This reference by Jesus about Elijah has since been understood by scholars as a reference to John the Baptizer, who had already died.

On another occasion when Jesus returned to Nazareth, where he was raised, he returned to the familiar synagogue of his home town. As he stood to read, a scroll was handed to Him. We read,

> the scroll of the prophet Isaiah was handed to him. Unrolling it, he found the place where it is written: "The Spirit of the LORD is on me, because he has anointed me to proclaim good news to the poor. He has sent me to proclaim freedom for the prisoners and recovery of sight for the blind, to set the oppressed free, to proclaim the year of the LORD's favor." Then he rolled up the scroll, gave it back to the attendant and sat down. The eyes of everyone in the synagogue were fastened on him. He began by saying to them, "Today this scripture is fulfilled in your hearing." (Luke 4:17-21)

Jesus was referring to the Old Testament prophecies, Isaiah 61:1-2, and 58:6. It was understood by the leaders in the synagogue and their ancestors as a reference to Isaiah who was predicting the

JESUS WAS (IS) SUBJECT TO SCRIPTURE

safe return of Israel after the exile to the promised land. Isaiah had been appointed to return with some more of the Jews who were still in captivity. Some of the remnant of Israel was believed to already have returned by the time of this prophecy.[1]

However, in this text, in Luke 4, Jesus declared to the amazement of those in the synagogue that day that "this prophecy is fulfilled in your hearing". Jesus knew this applied to Himself. He would do the proclaiming! This was His ministry.

Mark's account of Jesus announcing the coming of the good news of God to Israel urged a response that included repentance and faith. "After John was put in prison, Jesus went into Galilee, proclaiming the good news of God. 'The time has come,' he said. 'The kingdom of God has come near. Repent and believe the good news!'" (Mark 1:14-15). Here Jesus acknowledged He was the One who was to announce that the Kingdom of God has come near. It is near because of Himself, His ministry and the work set out before Him. The action in Mark's gospel, as compared to the other gospels, is noted as being much swifter, like let's 'get on with it'.

Jesus therefore obeyed the Word of God. He was subject to it. If some peoples' jaundiced view of Inspiration, earlier referenced, had some validity Jesus was subject to an errant, rather casually thrown-together 'word of people or Hebrew leadership'. Jesus would have been subject then to the will of people, not the Will of God. However, in all the details of His acts of redemption Jesus was subject to scripture, understood as God's Word. He obeyed it. It was His authority, the rule by which He lived. He came to do God's will not His own and not that of any human initiative.

Note how all of His life He did things because they were written—as if God had directly commanded. He saw fulfilled Old Testament prophecies about Himself. Such passages are found all over the Old Testament. For example,

> Do you think I cannot call on my Father, and he will at once put at my disposal more than twelve legions of angels? (see Psalm

91:11) But how then would the Scriptures be fulfilled that say it must happen in this way?" In that hour Jesus said to the crowd, "Am I leading a rebellion, that you have come out with swords and clubs to capture me? Every day I sat in the temple courts teaching, and you did not arrest me. But this has all taken place that the writings of the prophets might be fulfilled." (Matthew 26:53-56)

The prophet Daniel, according to some commentators, may have made reference to Jesus, as the son of man.

> In my vision at night I looked, and there before me was one like a son of man coming with the clouds of heaven. He approached the Ancient of Days and was led into his presence. He was given authority, glory and sovereign power; all nations and peoples of every language worshiped him. His dominion is an everlasting dominion that will not pass away, and his kingdom is one that will never be destroyed. (Daniel 7:13-14)

'Son of man' is translated from the Hebrew 'human being' for Daniel, but the former description, 'like a son of man' is picked up by the English translator since the New Testament later affirms who Daniel is likely seeing in his vision.[2]

In Mark's Gospel, Jesus had been challenged as to Who He was, by the High Priest, "Again the high priest asked him, 'Are you the Messiah, the Son of the Blessed One?'" (Mark 14:61b). Jesus had remained silent to the priest's first question in the context of the amazing claim made of the destruction of the temple in three days and then it being rebuild again, without human hands. (Mark 14:55-61a). Jesus picked up on this text located in Daniel 7:13 in His response: "'I am,' said Jesus, 'And you will see the Son of Man sitting at the right hand of the Mighty One and coming on the clouds of heaven'" (Mark 14:62).[3] Jesus referred to the description of what Daniel had seen and prophesied. Jesus picked up on the images of the Son of Man in Daniel. He would be given authority, glory and sovereign power and all the nations of every people would worship Him.

Jesus knew the Old Testament and the references which applied to the Son of Man, Himself. In response to being challenged by his disciples regarding their understanding of the coming again of Elijah, Jesus had referred to Elijah coming first, before the Messiah, according to the scribes. "See, I will send the prophet Elijah to you before that great and dreadful day of the LORD comes. He will turn the hearts of the parents to their children, and the hearts of the children to their parents; or else I will come and strike the land with total destruction." (Malachi 4:5-6) The disciples therefore questioned Jesus regarding his reference to Elijah. His response in Mark was that Elijah's prophesied return had occurred in John the Baptiser. See also Matthew 17:11-13. Prophesied in Isaiah 49:7 and 53:3, centuries earlier, were descriptions of what was to happen to the Messiah. Jesus may also have referred to Psalm 22:6 and 123:3-4 as He explained events about Himself in "In the same way the Son of Man is going to suffer at their hands" (Matthew 17:12b).[4]

JESUS' DEATH PROPHECIED

From the earliest days of His ministry years, this pending death and how it would come about was known to Him. Further, as the Cross came closer, Luke indicated that Jesus declared to the disciples the coming of his death for a third time.

> Jesus took the Twelve aside and told them, "We are going up to Jerusalem, and everything that is written by the prophets about the Son of Man will be fulfilled. He will be delivered over to the Gentiles. They will mock him, insult him and spit on him; they will flog him and kill him. On the third day he will rise again." The disciples did not understand any of this. Its meaning was hidden from them and they did not know what he was talking about. (Luke 18:31-34)

Jesus knew this Old Testament passage well and so indicated to the disciples, "Let's get going!" Jesus was subject to the scriptures, prophesied in the Old Testament regarding his life, death and resurrection. This all was fulfilled months after Jesus had indicated it to his disciples. These truths also worked out exactly as proclaimed centuries earlier. He predicted he would be arrested for this purpose.

Jesus knew the Cross was coming, for Him, as He ministered to the people and taught those who would listen. He knew the price to be paid - His death and resurrection - would free all humanity from sin's nature. Because of his death we could all be forgiven with the shedding of His blood. Paul later wrote to the Romans who too had become convinced of their own sinfulness, "But now that you have been set free from sin and have become slaves of God, the benefit you reap leads to holiness, and the result is eternal life. For the wages of sin is death, but the gift of God is eternal life in Christ Jesus our LORD" (Romans 6:22-23). Christ knew this was the purpose of His life and eventual death. It happened as John described this fact to all of us with these words, "So the soldiers took charge of Jesus. Carrying his own cross, he went out to the place of the Skull (which in Aramaic is called Golgotha). There they crucified him" (John 19:16b-18a).

Later Paul wrote to the Philippians concerning Jesus and what He believed about Himself: "And being found in appearance as a man, he humbled himself by becoming obedient to death—even death on a cross!" (Philippians 2:8). And finally, almost as a benediction, the writer to the Hebrews wrote to the Church, these words,

> Now may the God of peace, who through the blood of the eternal covenant brought back from the dead our Lord Jesus, that great Shepherd of the sheep, equip you with everything good for doing his will, and may he work in us what is pleasing to him, through Jesus Christ, to whom be glory for ever and ever. Amen. (Hebrews 13:20-2)

Here he makes reference to the covenant accepted by Israel, to tell the world around Who God is, and this covenant was fully completed in the work of the shedding of the blood of Christ Jesus.

This idea of prophecy fulfilled centuries later is unique, once again, to all written or oral religious discourse over the millennia amongst all peoples and tribes. Never has any religious literature, which is available in our hands today, been confirmed as to its truth and thus authority by prophecy both oral and written, centuries earlier. "It is written: 'And he was numbered with the transgressors'; and I tell you that this must be fulfilled in me. Yes, what is written about me is reaching its fulfillment." (Luke 22:37). Referring to: "Therefore I will give him a portion among the great, (or many) and he will divide the spoils with the strong, (or numerous) because he poured out his life unto death, and was numbered with the transgressors. For he bore the sin of many, and made intercession for the transgressors (Isaiah 53:12.) And lastly as referred to in the last chapter,

> He said to them, "This is what I told you while I was still with you: Everything must be fulfilled that is written about me in the Law of Moses, the Prophets and the Psalms." Then he opened their minds so they could understand the Scriptures. He told them, "This is what is written: The Messiah will suffer and rise from the dead on the third day, and repentance for the forgiveness of sins will be preached in his name to all nations, beginning at Jerusalem. You are witnesses of these things." (Luke 24:44-48)

Within these scripture references in the New Testament, the same Holy Spirit confirmed for us the Resurrection, witnessed by many, and tied it to the Old Testament prophets who wrote of these events centuries earlier. Jesus' view of the scriptures was seen to be confirmed by His submission to that work of the Holy Spirit in the acting out of those scriptures in His experience of life. Much of what was the fulfillment of Jesus actions, as prophesied, comes to us in the Biblical stories about Jesus' birth, death and resurrection. (Appendix A)

Jesus is, finally, subject to the scriptures that refer to the end times. He knew them, as we have them in the Bible, and looks forward to their completion. He told his disciples during his ministry before he went to the cross, "For the Son of Man is going to come in his Father's glory with his angels, and then he will reward each person according to what they have done" (Matthew 16:27). The Holy Spirit who is responsible for texts in the Old Testament that applied to Jesus, the same texts that confirm who He is in the New Testament, also through influence on the writer to the Revelation gave us references to the events that have not as yet taken place. This same Jesus, the Lamb who was slain on the Cross, who rose from the dead will someday return in Glory. "In a loud voice they were saying: 'Worthy is the Lamb, who was slain, to receive power and wealth and wisdom and strength and honor and glory and praise!'" (Revelation 5:12). And every person who ever lived will bow before Jesus, the Christ. Humanity will receive grace and peace

> And from Jesus Christ, who is the faithful witness, the firstborn from the dead, and the ruler of the kings of the earth. To him who loves us and has freed us from our sins by his blood, and has made us to be a kingdom and priests to serve his God and Father - to him be glory and power for ever and ever! Amen. "Look, he is coming with the clouds," and "every eye will see him, even those who pierced him"; and all peoples on earth "will mourn because of him." So shall it be! Amen. (Revelation 1:5-7)

So the Church awaits His return, whether we have passed on or are alive when He returns, in Glory.

Endnotes

1. Kelly, *Isaiah*, 362.
2. John Joseph Owens, *Daniel*, in The Broadman Bible Commentary, ed. Clifton J. Allen (Nashville, Broadman Press, 1971), Vol 6:424.
3. Owens, *Daniel*.
4. Henry Turlington, *Mark*, in The Broadman Bible Commentary, ed. Clifton J. Allen (Nashville, Broadman Press, 1971), Vol 8:389-391.

BY WHAT AUTHORITY

Chapter 7

THE ROLE OF PROPHECY IN SCRIPTURE

A significant means that the Holy Spirit has used to carry out the challenge, to inform humans about God's plan for all of us, is through the use of the prophet. Prophets in the Old Testament and to a limited extent in the New Testament had a continuing burden of proof, as to their role and authenticity. A prophet in the Old Testament was only affirmed by the community if what they spoke, which was later written, was validated in bringing the prophecy to fulfillment, even centuries later. We shall be reminded in this chapter that their authenticity or authority was also affirmed by the ongoing work of the Holy Spirit. The early prophetic writings, contained in the Bible only, were directed by God through the Holy Spirit. Over many centuries other human orators, writers and other self-proclaimed religious leaders, have sought to influence the various tribes, outside of and even within the Hebrew tribe, to follow after gods other than God the Father, Creator of heaven and earth.

We discover this dynamic, given to Israel by the prophet Moses, in his communication with the Father and Israel recorded in Deuteronomy.

> The nations you will dispossess listen to those who practice sorcery or divination. But as for you, the LORD your God has

not permitted you to do so. The LORD your God will raise up for you a prophet like me from among you, from your fellow Israelites. You must listen to him. For this is what you asked of the LORD your God at Horeb on the day of the assembly when you said, "Let us not hear the voice of the LORD our God nor see this great fire anymore, or we will die." The LORD said to me: "What they say is good. I will raise up for them a prophet like you from among their fellow Israelites, and I will put my words in his mouth. He will tell them everything I command him. I myself will call to account anyone who does not listen to my words that the prophet speaks in my name. But a prophet who presumes to speak in my name anything I have not commanded, or a prophet who speaks in the name of other gods, is to be put to death." You may say to yourselves, "How can we know when a message has not been spoken by the LORD?" If what a prophet proclaims in the name of the LORD does not take place or come true, that is a message the LORD has not spoken. That prophet has spoken presumptuously, so do not be alarmed". (Deuteronomy 18:14-22)

A number of points come from this biblical description of the role of the prophet, for Israel. These words describe what other nations had become dependent upon, among other things, to discover the mysteries of life and the world: sorcery and divination. Such behavior has not ceased to be seen as important to humanity to this day. Moses stated that the Father is not pleased with these types of searching and prohibits it. Instead the Father will establish, through the work of the Holy Spirit, a means or method of the communication of His will and pleasure. We have so far come to understand the influence of the Holy Spirit throughout scriptures and this role is most significant for establishing God's communication with all peoples and tribes.

It is clear to Moses as he communicates with the Israelites that this decision is for the betterment and encouragement of THAT nation. It is critical to distinguishing their means of understanding the

THE ROLE OF PROPHECY IN SCRIPTURE

world around them, from the various means available to the rest of humanity who have no knowledge of or connections with the Father. This lack of availability to the Father would one day, of course, be resolved by the work of Christ on the Cross and His Resurrection and eventual Return. This is the Gospel which runs throughout the Bible and is its main message to ALL peoples.

It is very important to note in this passage as well that a true prophet is always correct. This is the expectation of the Father and the clear work of the Holy Spirit. A person who gives a prophecy which proves to be inaccurate is not a true prophet. Do not listen to him or her. (Deuteronomy 18:20-22)

In the context of a family challenge to the leadership of Moses in the book of Numbers, the Lord intervened by defining the role of a prophet in Israel and similarly the Holy Spirit's view of this form of leadership. In Numbers 12:6-8 we read,

> He said, "Listen to my words: 'When there is a prophet among you, I, the LORD, reveal myself to them in visions, I speak to them in dreams. But this is not true of my servant Moses; he is faithful in all my house. With him I speak face to face, clearly and not in riddles; he sees the form of the LORD. Why then were you not afraid to speak against my servant Moses?'"

A distinction appears to be being made here by the Father, again through the Holy Spirit, between the role of a prophet as described and the role of Moses in his uniqueness amongst the leaders of Israel. Miriam and Aaron, Moses' sister and brother, were challenging the leadership of their brother. According to the text, the Lord called a family meeting to clarify Moses' distinctive role to that of the role of the prophet in Israel while the role and purpose of a prophet was being developed. By the time of the writing of first Samuel, prophets had a place in the life of Israel. (see1Samuel 10:9-11). Proof of the prophets' words meant he was recognized as the Lord's prophet.

Other local nations had definite problems with the prophets of Israel and their pronouncements. "While Jezebel was killing off the

LORD's prophets, Obadiah had taken a hundred prophets and hidden them in two caves, fifty in each, and had supplied them with food and water." (1 Kings 18:4) In this chapter one sees the work of the prophet Elijah and the respect given him by Obadiah, the Samarian palace administrator. See also 2 Chronicles 36:16. "But they mocked God's messengers, despised his words and scoffed at his prophets until the wrath of the LORD was aroused against his people and there was no remedy." In this context, Judah had moved away from the Lord and become unfaithful to Him. (2 Chronicles 36:14) The culture around had, once again, influenced them away from following the Father's will. Similarity the Church is aware of cultural influences that move believers away from the Scriptures and we can also become unfaithful. Some things repeat themselves throughout history and the Holy Spirit is yet active towards the imperative of using the Bible to challenge the North American and worldwide Church.

The biblical authors, who describe the role of prophets, did not necessarily see the prophets as being able to prophesy the future but rather as persons who could communicate with God. Therefore, we can come to realize that prophets played a significant role in the life of the Hebrew people who the Father had earlier called and commissioned to tell the world around them Who He is. To challenge Israel with such a calling, without **some means** of knowing what the Father was about, would seem to have been cruel and virtually impossible. Throughout human history individual men and women have sought to understand the things of the world around them, both seen and not seen. Every tribe on earth, that has been studied, has recorded the efforts of elders, including oral traditions, to understand the world in which they live. Signs have been sought, with patience. But what means does the Father choose to use to communicate to all humankind? The prophet.

Certainly, over the history of humanity, elements of the creation have influenced 'ideas' about a God, a Creator. Humans have paid attention to that which is around them, from the beginning. Signs have been sought in the sky, stars, the large and the small; all have been influential in seeking to help humanity understand if there is a Creator and what He might be like. But to challenge a specific nation to the task of being the 'witnesses' to the Father's plan for salvation? Really? By what authority? The authority of a true, always right, biblical prophet, as described within the Bible. The Father gave prophets to Israel, among other things, to assist them in that unique and common desire to search the nature and complexity of the world around.

There were also false prophets in the Old Testament so Israel could learn to understand the significance of the difference, and what to do about that falsity. In Jeremiah 28:8-9 an experience of a false prophet, one where the prophecy of any sort does not end up being true, is demonstrated. Hananiah brought a word of prophecy in the presence of the priests and in the house of the Lord. In the text, Jeremiah gave a definition of a true prophet. In verses 8-9 we read, "From early times the prophets who preceded you and me have prophesied war, disaster and plague against many countries and great kingdoms. But the prophet who prophesies peace will be recognized as one truly sent by the LORD only if his prediction comes true." Following this word from Jeremiah in chapter 28, Hananiah broke the yoke that Jeremiah had worn about his neck indicating that it represented or was a symbol of the subjection that the king of Babylon had placed upon the Jews. Hananiah had falsely prophesied that the yoke of Babylon would be broken within 2 years. Jeremiah, after later hearing from the Lord that this would not be the case in the near future, came to Hananiah away from the presence of the priests and people and challenged his false prophecy, whereupon Hananiah soon died. (Jeremiah 28:15-17)

With such a powerful example of communication between the Divine and Israel, it was not surprising that prophecy could be falsified, be untrue, not coming from the Lord. Such was the pressure in Israel to be careful to whom they listened. Above all, in the context of the use of the prophet by the Lord, was the call on the people to love the Lord God with 'all your heart' first, foremost and eternally. Moses gave such an illustration of priority in Deuteronomy 13.

> If a prophet, or one who foretells by dreams, appears among you and announces to you a sign or wonder, and if the sign or wonder spoken of takes place, and the prophet says, "Let us follow other gods" (gods you have not known) "and let us worship them," you must not listen to the words of that prophet or dreamer. The LORD your God is testing you to find out whether you love him with all your heart and with all your soul. It is the LORD your God you must follow, and him you must revere. Keep his commands and obey him; serve him and hold fast to him. That prophet or dreamer must be put to death for inciting rebellion against the LORD your God, who brought you out of Egypt and redeemed you from the land of slavery. That prophet or dreamer tried to turn you from the way the LORD your God commanded you to follow. You must purge the evil from among you. (Deuteronomy 13:1-5)

These words are given to us, the Church, because over human history many have approached tribes or individuals with a false call, not originating from the Holy Spirit, challenging them to some form of leadership, worship or religious ceremony. False prophecy leads people to an imagined sense of Who the Father is and moves them in a different direction than the Bible illuminates and has done so for millennia.

Prophets are both male and female in the scriptural record. "Then Miriam the prophet, Aaron's sister, took a timbrel in her hand, and all the women followed her, with timbrels and dancing. Miriam sang to them: 'Sing to the LORD, for he is highly exalted. Both horse and driver he has hurled into the sea'" (Exodus 15:20-21). Further we can read of Deborah "Now Deborah, a prophet, the wife of Lappidoth, was leading Israel at that time. She held court under the Palm of Deborah between Ramah and Bethel in the hill country of Ephraim, and the Israelites went up to her to have their disputes decided" (Judges 4:4-5). In Luke we read, "There was also a prophet, Anna, the daughter of Penuel, of the tribe of Asher. She was very old"

(Luke 2:36a), and further in Acts, "Leaving the next day, we reached Caesarea and stayed at the house of Philip the evangelist, one of the Seven. He had four unmarried daughters who prophesied" (Acts 21:8-9).

As with the New Testament, there are no restrictions on gender for prophets. In Ezekiel 13, the Holy Spirit goes after the false prophets who were female just as He goes after the false prophets who were male. A standard is set in the Old Testament for all prophecy. It must be true and confirmed. False prophecy did occur in Israel. As one reads that chapter we notice, "The word of the Lord came to me: 'Son of man, prophesy against the prophets of Israel who are now prophesying.' Say to those who prophesy out of their own imagination: 'Hear the word of the Lord! This is what the Sovereign Lord says: Woe to the foolish prophets who follow their own spirit and have seen nothing!'" (Ezekiel 13:1-3), and further, "Now, son of man, set your face against the daughters of your people who prophesy out of their own imagination. Prophesy against them" (Ezekiel 13:17).

As an important aside, there are also several references in the New Testament to the Gifts of the Spirit. These too have no reference to gender but are critical to the Holy Spirit's work in the Church. An example is seen in 1 Corinthians 12:1-11. (See also Romans 12:6-8; Ephesians 4:11-13). All believers are gifted through the work of the Holy Spirit. The gifts benefit the local and worldwide Church.

Peter helpfully made reference to his view of prophecy,

> We also have the prophetic message as something completely reliable, and you will do well to pay attention to it, as to a light shining in a dark place, until the day dawns and the morning star rises in your hearts. Above all, you must understand that no prophecy of Scripture came about by the prophet's own interpretation of things. For prophecy never had its origin in the human will, but prophets, though human, spoke from God as they were carried along by the Holy Spirit." (2 Peter 1:19-21)

Peter also agreed here with Jesus' view of the scriptures.

A true prophet, therefore, was called and equipped by God, empowered by the Holy Spirit to perform his or her job—to speak God's message, confront people with sin, warn of coming judgment and the consequences if God's people refused to repent and obey. As "seers," prophets also brought a message of hope and future blessing for those who walk in obedience. They also confirmed the work of salvation history for the benefit of humanity. The biblical authors, inspired by the Holy Spirit, did not necessarily see the prophet as being able to prophesy the future as earlier noted, but rather as persons with whom God could communicate.

HOW PROPHECY TIES IN THE OLD AND NEW TESTAMENTS

As explained earlier a true prophet of God was consistent and eventually shown to be correct. The significance of the Old Testament prophet, for our consideration, is that it was often years or even centuries before a prophecy was seen to have been fulfilled or understood to having been fulfilled. These many confirmations of prophecy declare, indicate and confirm the uniqueness of the Bible over any other sacred declarations and written work by recognized spiritual leaders throughout human history. Biblical prophets pointed the way to Jesus, the Messiah and showed all people their need of his salvation. Some have attempted to make a strong connection between the role of a prophet and the idea of telling the future. They believe that a prophet is someone who makes (or made, in the case of the Bible) a lot of predictions about what's going to happen.

There is certainly truth to that idea. Prophecies recorded in Scripture that deal with future events were written or spoken by the prophets. For example, Daniel predicted the rise and fall of several empires in the ancient world, including the Medo-Persian alliance, the Greeks led by Alexander the Great, and the Roman Empire (see Daniel 7:1-14).

Most significant for our purposes here are the prophecies that are considered Messianic. They predicted the coming of the Messiah centuries before He arrived. Isaiah predicted that Jesus would be born to a virgin. "Therefore the LORD himself will give you a sign: The virgin will conceive and give birth to a son, and will call him Immanuel." (Isaiah 7:14) The follow-up confirmation of the prophet's writing is discovered in two passages in the New Testament, recorded 7 centuries later in Matthew and Luke. "All this took place to fulfill what the Lord had said through the prophet: 'The virgin will conceive and give birth to a son, and they will call him Immanuel' (which means "God with us")" (Matthew 1:22-23)

And,

> In the sixth month of Elizabeth's pregnancy, God sent the angel Gabriel to Nazareth, a town in Galilee, to a virgin pledged to be married to a man named Joseph, a descendant of David. The virgin's name was Mary. The angel went to her and said, "Greetings, you who are highly favored! The LORD is with you." Mary was greatly troubled at his words and wondered what kind of greeting this might be. But the angel said to her, "Do not be afraid, Mary; you have found favor with God. You will conceive and give birth to a son, and you are to call him Jesus. (Luke 1:26-31)

The place of the birth of the Messiah was prophesied, even the right Bethlehem amongst several options at the time, in Micah 5:2. "But you, Bethlehem Ephrathah, though you are small among the clans of Judah, out of you will come for me one who will be ruler over Israel, whose origins are from of old, from ancient times." It was fulfilled and recorded centuries later in Matthew and Luke. "After Jesus was born in Bethlehem in Judea, during the time of King Herod, Magi from the east came to Jerusalem and asked, 'Where is the one who has been born king of the Jews? We saw his star when it rose and have come to worship him'" (Matthew 2:1-2; see also Luke 2:4-7).

In Acts 3:17-22 we read, in further reference to prophecy, that this Jesus, being the expected Messiah, would eventually suffer.

Now, fellow Israelites, I know that you acted in ignorance, as did your leaders. But this is how God fulfilled what he had foretold through all the prophets, saying that his Messiah would suffer. Repent, then, and turn to God, so that your sins may be wiped out, that times of refreshing may come from the LORD, and that he may send the Messiah, who has been appointed for you - even Jesus. Heaven must receive him until the time comes for God to restore everything, as he promised long ago through his holy prophets. For Moses said, "The LORD your God will raise up for you a prophet like me from among your own people; you must listen to everything he tells you."

Here, in the New Testament, centuries after Moses prophesied that another prophet would be raised up, the apostle Peter who travelled with Jesus and witnessed his crucifixion and resurrection, spoke to the Israelites, as one of them. He tied the significance of prophecy in the Old Testament to the events being recorded in the New Testament. Peter, here inspired by the Holy Spirit now released to the Church, referred to other prophecies that referenced the suffering of the Messiah. In Isaiah 53 there is a description of the suffering of the Messiah, the suffering servant, and how he will be rejected by Israel. "We all, like sheep, have gone astray, each of us has turned to our own way; and the LORD has laid on him the iniquity of us all" (Isaiah 53:6). Throughout the Old Testament, prophecy refers to the One who will come to the rescue of Israel, in a more permanent, eternal way. "But you, Bethlehem Ephrathah, though you are small among the clans of Judah, out of you will come for me one who will be ruler over Israel, whose origins are from of old, from ancient times" (Micah 5:2).

Peter and other New Testament writers referred to the return of the Messiah at some future date which was also prophesied in the Old Testament but not yet accomplished. The Gospel writers, under the influence of the Holy Spirit pick up the theme of the Messiah. And many people have attempted throughout history to emulate this figure. Jesus warned,

Watch out that no one deceives you. For many will come in my name, claiming, "I am the Messiah," and will deceive many. You will hear of wars and rumors of wars, but see to it that you are not alarmed. Such things must happen, but the end is still to come. Nation will rise against nation, and kingdom against kingdom. There will be famines and earthquakes in various places. All these are the beginning of birth pains." (Matthew 24:4-8)

Then later in Matthew, "Then will appear the sign of the Son of Man in heaven. And then all the peoples of the earth will mourn when they see the Son of Man coming on the clouds of heaven, with power and great glory. And he will send his angels with a loud trumpet call, and they will gather his elect from the four winds, from one end of the heavens to the other" (Matthew 24:30-31).

During His ministry Jesus himself referred to His future return, "And if I go and prepare a place for you, I will come back and take you to be with me that you also may be where I am" (John 14:3). Or regarding His eventual return, "For the Son of Man is going to come in his Father's glory with his angels, and then he will reward each person according to what they have done. 'Truly I tell you, some who are standing here will not taste death before they see the Son of Man coming in his kingdom'" (Matthew 16:27-8). Many standing there would see His Resurrected Glory. We read that Jesus after once again referring to authority given by the Father, returned to heaven. "After he said this, he was taken up before their very eyes, and a cloud hid him from their sight. They were looking intently up into the sky as he was going, when suddenly two men dressed in white stood beside them. 'Men of Galilee,' they said, 'why do you stand here looking into the sky? This same Jesus, who has been taken from you into heaven, will come back in the same way you have seen him go into heaven'" (Acts 1:9-11). What He prophesied in Matthew 16:28 shortly came to pass.

In Revelation we read what is yet to happen, "Look, he is coming with the clouds, and every eye will see him, even those who pierced him; and all peoples on earth will mourn because of him. So shall it be! Amen" (Revelation 1:7). And further, "Look, I am coming soon! My reward is with me, and I will give to each person according to what they have done. I am the Alpha and the Omega, the First and the Last, the Beginning and the End" (Revelation 22:12-13). Some of the prophecies in the Old and New Testaments, while true, have not yet been fulfilled. This is an aspect of biblical prophecy and a prophet's role.

But telling the future was not the major role of the Old Testament prophets as already suggested. In fact, those prophecies that related to future events were more of a side effect of their main role and function. The primary role of the prophets in the Bible was to speak with the people about the words and will of God in their specific situations. The prophets served as God's megaphones, declaring whatever God commanded them to say. And the Father's overall interest and challenge by giving them prophets was that Israel would continue to "tell the world Who God is".

What's also interesting is that God Himself defined the role and function of the prophets at the beginning of Israel's history as a nation, "I will raise up for them a prophet like you from among their fellow Israelites, and I will put my words in his mouth. He will tell them everything I command him. I myself will call to account anyone who does not listen to my words that the prophet speaks in my name" (Deuteronomy 18:18-19). A prophet in the Bible then was someone who spoke the words of God to people who needed to hear them. This is an important definition of a prophet, for our consideration.

Research by Mary Fairchild[1] has indicated that there are 44 such Messianic prophesies which are recorded on the Old Testament and confirmed in the New Testament. An interesting illustration about the probability of **just eight** of these prophesies of Jesus being correctly fulfilled comes from Peter Stoner[2] who indicated, "The chance of eight prophecies all being fulfilled correctly is 1 in 10^{17} power." Stoner gives an illustration that helps visualize the magnitude of such odds.

Suppose that we take 10^{17} silver dollars and lay them on the face of the state of Texas. They will cover all of the state two feet deep. Now mark one of these silver dollars and stir the whole mass thoroughly, all over the State. Blindfold a person and tell them that they can travel as far as they wish, but they must pick up one silver dollar and say that this is the right one. What chance would they have of getting the right one? Just the same chance that the prophets would have had of writing these eight prophecies and having them all come true in any one man, from their day to that present time, providing they wrote using their own wisdom. The mathematical improbability of 300, or just 44, or even just **eight** fulfilled prophesies of Jesus stands as interesting evidence to his Messiahship.

It also affirms the occasional work of the Holy Spirit in using prophets in predictive role. The illustration confirms the Holy Spirit's involvement not only in creating human history and bringing it to completion but also to affirm His activity in the Bible's unique significance, for humanity. The authority of the Bible is affirmed by the work of the prophets over many centuries and even to today, as influenced by the ongoing work of God's Holy Spirit.

Biblical scholarship has intimated that there are more than 300 Old Testament prophetic Scriptures completed during the life of Jesus. Circumstances such as his birthplace, lineage, method of execution and resurrection were beyond His control and could not have been accidentally or deliberately fulfilled. Further, but out of the scope of this book, is a prophecy from Zechariah which has had influence on the interpretation of the significance of the Bible, in a more recent time. He prophesied, "This is what the Lord Almighty says: 'I will save my people from the countries of the east and the west. I will bring them back to live in Jerusalem; they will be my people, and I will be faithful and righteous to them as their God'" (Zechariah 8:7-8). In 1947 Israel, in cooperation with the allies in the West after the second world war, returned to the land of their forefathers, as promised by God centuries earlier.

A further example of the role of prophecy is noted in Zechariah 9:9. Zion or Israel is called by the prophet to greet her king who brings peace and dominion [3] "Rejoice greatly, Daughter Zion! Shout, Daughter Jerusalem! See, your king comes to you, righteous and victorious, lowly and riding on a donkey, on a colt, the foal of a donkey." The Holy Spirit influences Matthew to see Jesus' action, centuries later, as a fulfillment of this Old Testament text. Near the end of His ministry, Jesus comes into Jerusalem riding on a donkey and Israel celebrates. "This took place to fulfill what was spoken through the prophet: Say to Daughter Zion, 'See, your king comes to you, gentle and riding on a donkey, and on a colt, the foal of a donkey'" (Matthew 21:4-5; see also Luke 19:28-44).

As already indicated, John the Baptizer's appearance during Jesus' ministry was influential in illustrating the fulfilling of the role of prophecy in scripture. In Malachi, the prophet related an event in the future that would come to pass. "'I will send my messenger, who will prepare the way before me. Then suddenly the Lord you are seeking will come to his temple; the messenger of the covenant, whom you desire, will come,' says the Lord Almighty" (Malachi 3:1). At John's request, his disciples inquired of Jesus about whether He was the expected Messiah. In giving them an answer, Luke picked up on this, referring to Malachi's text and quoting Jesus answer. (See Luke 7:24-28).

So centuries later Luke recognized, from his knowledge of the Old Testament, that John was the one to which Malachi was referring. This confirms, once more, a role of prophecy in scripture.

And lastly consider the text in Acts 2 where Peter referred to the Holy Spirit's action at Pentecost. After the early church's experience, the apostle addressed the crowd who were all amazed and asked, "Amazed and perplexed, they asked one another, 'What does this mean?'" (Acts 2:12). Peter tied the experience to an Old Testament prophet, Joel, given centuries earlier. (See Acts 2:16-21). The role of prophecy continued to affirm the calling of the Church to the work of telling the world around them, Who God, the Father is.

In the meantime, students of scripture and others seeking a faith rightly struggle with writings and oracles produced over centuries, that proport to be 'truth' for all people. Prophetic truths are needed to interpret and attempt to explain things like: the purpose of a created humanity on this earth if there is one, our relationship to one another as humans living on a beautiful organized and intentionally structured planet and what each of our eternal futures could look like. The Father's love and Creation of our 'home' had the intention of restoring our relationship to Himself, eventually. This was the challenge to Israel: tell the world around you Who I Am. The Father chose to assist in that telling through the network of prophecy, imbedded in the Word of God, the Bible. So, the prophets acted in faith and determination to communicate as they were able the care, love and purposes of the Father.

Fulfilled prophecy is key to understanding the structural integrity of the complete Biblical text. Woven throughout the text, from Genesis to Revelation, is a fabric of spoken and eventually written material that continues to tie historical events together. If prophets spoke and the matters to which they referred were false, this argument would be futile. Much of the Bible could be challenged as anthropology, archeology and other scientific endeavors have sought to do with much of its written religious material, over the millennia. The truth of prophecy in the Hebrew and Greek biblical record has succeeded in affirming the work of Christ as Redeemer for all humankind, not just for the Hebrew tribe. The successfully prophesied acts of Christ's life, death and resurrection and the unanswered prophecy within those same scriptures that refer to the 'end times', continue to authenticate the faith of the Church, which awaits the consummation of all history.

Throughout the writings of the New Testament the element of prophecy continued to influence the faithful in the way the Father desired to communicate and continues to communicate, to the Church. This is important to note because in much of the Old Testament prophecy, to which this book refers, there is much more one could consider that relates to prophetic fulfillment in the New Testament, as revealed centuries later. All scripture has been inspired by the work of the Holy Spirit, Who used prophecy. This is a key concept in understanding the ongoing place of the Bible in the world of religious writings, which are so prevalent in these more recent centuries. The Bible is the plumb line, defining what is true and what is false. Prophetic declarations inspired by the Holy Spirit using ordinary followers, bring confirmation of the Bible's significance to humanity.

Whether the Bible is like any other religious writings and/or verbal declarations or not, one must consider the Authority that has created religious experience and religious following: that has attempted to create an affirmation of a valid faith. So far, we have seen through the work of the Holy Spirit, over all time, that the Bible stands out as unique, given the work of prophecy embedded in the text; prophetic work that has been confirmed time and time again as true and therefore **authoritative**. Again, it is the plumb line by which one can measure all other religious material, ever spoken or written.

Endnotes

1. Mary Fairchild, *44 Prophecies Jesus Fulfilled,* in Book of Bible Lists, D. Story (Peabody, MA: Rose Publishing, 1977), 79-80.
2. Peter Stoner, *Science Speaks* (Chicago: Moody Publishers, 1958).
3. John D. W. Watts, *Zechariah* in in The Broadman Bible Commentary, ed. Clifton J. Allen (Nashville: Broadman Press, 1971), Vol 7: 339.

BY WHAT AUTHORITY

Chapter 8

THE ROLE OF THE HOLY SPIRIT IN SCRIPTURE

An understanding, and brief review, of the work of the Holy Spirit throughout the ages will assist in coming to grips with the Authority of the Bible in the light of all other writings, which have influenced humanity for religious and spiritual purposes. The Holy Spirit or Spirit is referred to 101 times in the Bible. The Holy Spirit used and continues to use humans in the communication of the Will of the Father to all people. As inspired through the writing of the epistle of Peter, we understand that the Holy Spirit used prophets who "spoke from God" to humanity. No other religious writing to this date has claimed this strategy, much less even attempted to demonstrate it. It appears that the Holy Spirit has not used this strategy in any other religious writings or tribal oral traditions. The Holy Spirit used people, men and women, to communicate His plan for the reclamation of humankind from sin, failure and guilt. The inspired scriptures, proven factual through prophecy fulfilled and yet to be fulfilled, leads us to come to grips with the authenticity of these words in comparison to all the words written in every spiritual and religious writing over the millennia, from earliest Asian writings to those of the more recent centuries. Therefore, the prophet Isaiah can claim, under the influence of this same Holy Spirit, millennia ago, "the word of our God endures forever" (Isaiah 40:8).

The Holy Spirit appears, in some manner, in nearly every book of the Bible. In Genesis 1:1-2. "In the beginning God created the heavens and the earth. Now the earth was formless and empty, darkness was over the surface of the deep, and the Spirit of God was hovering over the waters." The Spirit of God was hovering over the waters at the Creation. The doctrine of the Trinity has been and will continue to be more complicated to understand than one would like.

There have been many illustrations used in an attempt to explain the Trinity, from a human perspective. One favorite is, I am a husband, father, brother, as well as other roles actually, but 3 roles are sufficient to understand the illustration - that I function in each of those roles, from time to time. Sometimes I function in more than one role at the same time. However, I am still only one person. At times I clearly function as a husband. Other times I clearly function as a father, likewise a brother. God the Father, God the Son and God the Spirit each function in their roles from time to time but God is One. Each Persona of the Trinity has a clear delineation as to purpose as explained within the scriptures. This is clearly biblical theology even though it is complicated for many of us to fully explain and understand.

Over the waters of the creation the Holy Spirit hovered in a purpose still not completely clear, yet the Spirit was functioning in that role and it is recorded so in this text. God the Father was also functioning at the same instance, for purposes explained in the first chapters of Genesis. The doctrine of creation has always been an interesting challenge for a preaching pastor. My role has been involved with coming to understand the complexities of the Genesis account of the creation. But what if, for example, the meaning of the Hebrew word for 'day' in the concept of the Holy Spirit's view, has little to do with earth time? Recently I heard one of our astronauts who had been on a space capsule refer to 'moon time'. 'Time' outside of the earth's influence is a meaningless concept. There is no 'earth' time in the universe.

The astronaut's comment affirmed for me that the concept of

time in Genesis, as far as days of creation, might just be different than we tend to think or experience. For me, the idea challenges the age-old arguments about the 'time' it took to create the universe, earth and human beings. Further, just for consideration, sitting in my garden patio I have wondered, as many of you no doubt have, watching as the bees come and go searching for the right flowers to obtain pollen, which came first? Was it the bees that pollinate the flowers or the flowers themselves and later, the bees? They both need each other, it seems to me. One process cannot exist without the other and likely did not. Seems to refer to a design rather than an evolutionary blunder or freak chance.

The Holy Spirit moves the story in the Bible book by book. The orators and writers played roles of which they were not familiar or even aware. Only in the conclusion of the canonization and the eventual printing of the Bible does humanity more fully come to grips with the plan and purpose of the Bible. It includes some history even though the Bible was not intended to be an historical document. However, where it refers to history it continues to be proven correct.

Over the centuries the science of archeology, referred to earlier, has contributed to confirmation of locations and events mentioned in the biblical record. An argument against the authority of scripture, for ages, has been that when the Bible seems to have been demonstrated to be in error over locations or events, its authenticity must be challenged. Such claims are to be heard and appreciated. The 'contest' as it were for affirming the work of the Holy Spirit in giving us the whole Bible is not really important to the Holy Spirit. In time the truth of the Bible is revealed, text by text. Locations and events continue to be discovered by the work of archeologists and other students studying our earth's history. Fascinating studies on DNA have come to light since the early 1950's.[1] One can google many topics today regarding the work of intelligent design theorists. Our education systems worldwide continue to work outside of the affirmation of the Bible and its significance, challenging human belief systems.

To further follow up the work of the Holy Spirit in the Bible,

He seems to demonstrate a human-like behaviour although He is neither female nor male. The Bible indicates the Holy Spirit can be grieved, "Yet they rebelled and grieved his Holy Spirit" (Isaiah 63:10). The Spirit could be withdrawn from humanity. In Genesis the Spirit indicated that there was an apparent built-in limit to the Father's enduring love. Already the Father knew humankind would be corrupted. Then the LORD said, "My Spirit will not contend with humans forever, for they are mortal; [corrupted] their days will be a hundred and twenty years" (Genesis 6:3). The Holy Spirit gave us another illustration in Israel's king Saul. "Now the Spirit of the LORD had departed from Saul, and an evil spirit from the LORD tormented him" (1 Samuel 16:14). And in an opposite response from Saul, king David also sinned and experienced the withdrawal of the Presence of the Spirit. We read of his plea, "Do not cast me from your presence or take your Holy Spirit from me" (Psalm 51:11). For inspiration see more of David's response in Psalm 51:1-19. Here David was aware of the work of the Holy Spirit, acting on the behalf of the Father.

Throughout the Old Testament record God, the Father, through the Holy Spirit's words to the prophets, would determine the restoration of Israel, rescuing them from the power and control of nations not following the Lord. Also, He will rescue them from the control over humankind, by the evil one. The Holy Spirit will eventually be poured out upon Israel. "I will no longer hide my face from them, for I will pour out my Spirit on the people of Israel, declares the Sovereign LORD" (Ezekiel 39:29). Eventually a Spirit of grace and supplication will be poured out upon Jerusalem when the Son is pierced on the Cross. "And I will pour out on the house of David and the inhabitants of Jerusalem a spirit of grace and supplication. They will look on me, the one they have pierced, and they will mourn for him as one mourns for an only child, and grieve bitterly for him as one grieves for a firstborn son" (Zechariah 12:10).

The prophet further indicated that the Spirit will be poured out on ALL people. "And afterward, I will pour out my Spirit on all people. Your sons and daughters will prophesy, your old men will dream dreams, your young men will see visions (Joel 2:28). The promise to Israel when their Redeemer comes to Zion will be an evidence of the Spirit that will not depart from them. "'As for me, this is my covenant with them,' says the LORD. 'My Spirit, who is on you, will not depart from you, and my words that I have put in your mouth will always be on your lips, on the lips of your children and on the lips of their descendants-from this time on and forever,' says the LORD" (Isaiah 59:21).

Throughout the Old Testament the Holy Spirit is active in working with the people of Israel, the Father's chosen, those who were originally challenged to 'tell the world Who God is'. Their ultimate failure to carry out that challenge was known by the Father from the beginning, even as He created the universe. Such failure is not to be discounted but is to be recognized as the exact same nature of all of us to fail the Father, in our actions towards Him and others. Every person, male, female, of every race, every color, with every ability have all sinned. God the Father has been in the business of redemption from the very beginning. The Holy Spirit, so aware of this fact, built the expectation of a Savior, a Redeemer, that would come. He did so throughout the Old Testament in anticipation of the New Testament events. Within the Old Testament the Holy Spirit, speaking through the writers of the material, was already preparing for the answer to humanity's bent to sinfulness. The Answer was always coming. In the context of new life, fertility and peace Isaiah said, "till the Spirit is poured on us from on high, and the desert becomes a fertile field, and the fertile field seems like a forest" (Isaiah 32:15). David's words speaking through the Holy Spirit in the Old Testament in Psalm 110:1 is confirmed by the New Testament witness to the people of Israel. David himself, speaking by the Holy Spirit, declared, "The LORD said to my LORD: 'Sit at my right hand until I put your enemies under your feet'" (Mark 12:36).

In the New Testament we read that the baby within Elizabeth's womb, leapt at the sound of the voice of Jesus' mother who was also pregnant with Jesus. Elizabeth was then filled with the Holy Spirit.

"When Elizabeth heard Mary's greeting, the baby (John) leaped in her womb, and Elizabeth was filled with the Holy Spirit" (Luke 1:41). The Holy Spirit remains active from the time of Creation to the time of the creation of the Church in the New Testament period. This Holy Spirit Who moved the orators and writers of the Old Testament is active in the process of bringing the completion of God's eternal plan of salvation to all peoples, through the orators and writers of the New Testament. The miraculous conception of Jesus' birth was the work of the Holy Spirit. The angel answered, "The Holy Spirit will come on you, and the power of the Most High will overshadow you. So the holy one to be born will be called the Son of God" (Luke 1:35).

It is important to note that an angel is credited, by Dr. Luke the writer of this gospel, for indicating to Mary the source of the pregnancy. By what authority does this information prove valid? The authority of the angel's message comes from the previous work of the same Holy Spirit who indicated, in prophecy in the Old Testament centuries earlier, that these events would someday take place. Any angel that speaks sacred text must have credentialed Authority to speak, and always be correct, as were the true prophets of the Old and New Testaments. What is spoken here must agree with the Holy Spirit inspired Old Testament.

In the same context John's father, Zechariah, was filled with the Holy Spirit which connected his experience to the ongoing work of the Holy Spirit's prophetic actions throughout the Old Testament times. (See Luke 1:67-75). Matthew ties the Old Testament promises and prophecies with the New Testament activity of the coming of the Christ child. In Matthew's gospel we read, "This is how the birth of Jesus the Messiah came about: His mother Mary was pledged to be married to Joseph, but before they came together, she was found to be pregnant through the Holy Spirit" (Matthew 1:18; see also Matthew 1:20).

Then tying later events to the development of the fledging Church, the Holy Spirit emphasizes the work of John the Baptizer by quoting John who baptizes Israelites "I baptize you with water for repentance. But after me comes one who is more powerful than I, whose sandals I am not worthy to carry. He will baptize you with the Holy Spirit and fire" (Matthew 3:11). John makes reference in this text to Jesus, who comes later. The activity of the Holy Spirit continues through the work of John the Baptizer as the New Testament record of the 'Church' is established, as promised over and over in the Old Testament through the prophets.

Evidence of His influence can be seen in a number of texts that prepared the Church for development and growth. Of particular note are the three references that indicate the only sin of humankind that will not be forgiven. Over human history, running parallel to the development of the Bible, by the Holy Spirit's work and influence, are rules, laws and other human created oral and written material that are suggested to supersede the biblical record; even disagreeing with the Scriptures. An example of the only unforgiveable sin is found in these three New Testament texts. "Anyone who speaks a word against the Son of Man will be forgiven, but anyone who speaks against the Holy Spirit will not be forgiven, either in this age or in the age to come" (Matthew 12:32; Mark 3:29; Luke12:10). It is such a heartbreak for a pastor to be confronted by some believers and even pastoral peers who imagine other types of sins that people are wont to do and who then add these types of sins to their lists. There are no LISTS of unforgiveable sins. Just one. That's why we have the Bible, the plumb line, to critique all other religion's ideology.

Further involvement of the Holy Spirit in the New Testament is noted in Luke 2:25. Now there was a man in Jerusalem called Simeon, who was righteous and devout. He was waiting for the consolation of Israel, and the Holy Spirit was on him. Simeon is referred to as righteous and devout although not referred to as a prophet. Jesus had been taken to the temple in Jerusalem, which was a Hebrew custom of purification rites and consecration to the Lord for each male child. (see Luke 2:22-35). There Simeon, to whom it was revealed by this same Holy Spirit that he would live until he saw the Lord's Messiah (Luke 2:26), encountered Jesus about whom he had been given the revelation. The Holy Spirit is all over this experience of Simeon.

There had been an expectation, for centuries, of the coming of the Messiah. As John the baptizer was becoming popular with the Hebrew people and was immersing those Jews who repented of their sinful lifestyle, he was challenged according to Luke's account, of being that promised Messiah. "The people were waiting expectantly and were all wondering in their hearts if John might possibly be the Messiah. John answered them all, 'I baptize you with water. But one who is more powerful than I will come, the straps of whose sandals I am not worthy to untie. He will baptize you with the Holy Spirit and fire'" (Luke 3:15-16). Here the Holy Spirit is tied to the commencement of the Church through this Jesus, a child born earlier in Bethlehem, as prophesied. He will be the Good News about which the nation of Israel has been waiting, for centuries. Just a little later Luke indicated Jesus' connection to the ongoing work of the Holy Spirit. "When all the people were being baptized, Jesus was baptized too. And as he was praying, heaven was opened and the Holy Spirit descended on him in bodily form like a dove. And a voice came from heaven: 'You are my Son, whom I love; with you I am well pleased'" (Luke 3:21-22).

This action by John has been understood classically in Christian theology as a very important point concerning baptism. Jesus was baptised by John who was baptizing Jews publicly indicating they had asked forgiveness for their sins, privately. This preached message was resonating with the Jews. But Jesus, according to the New Testament was sinless. The apostle Peter in his Holy Spirit inspired writing, much later, in reflecting on Jesus' sinless life noted, "He committed no sin, and no deceit was found in his mouth" (1 Peter 2:22). Peter was aware of these words from the prophet Isaiah in 53:9 and by the influence of this same Holy Spirit took references to the suffering servant and applied them to Jesus' life.

Further in 2 Corinthians 5:21 the apostle Paul noted, "God made him who had no sin to be sin for us, so that in him we might become the righteousness of God." The Holy Spirit inspired writer to the

Hebrews wrote,

> Therefore, since we have a great high priest who has ascended into heaven, Jesus the Son of God, let us hold firmly to the faith we profess. For we do not have a high priest who is unable to empathize with our weaknesses, but we have one who has been tempted in every way, just as we are-yet he did not sin. Let us then approach God's throne of grace with confidence, so that we may receive mercy and find grace to help us in our time of need. (Hebrews 4:14-16)

He noted, as an encouragement to the Church, that Jesus the Christ was tempted in every way that humanity is, yet without sin. [see also 1 John 3:5, John 8:29]. Therefore, Jesus' baptism by John was carried out as a challenge for the Church to follow rather than as a public recognition of a confession of Jesus' sins.

Jesus Himself was possessed by the Holy Spirit (see Luke 4:1; 10:21; Mark 1:8). Jesus said, according to Luke, that this promise of the Holy Spirit in one's life is also for the Church's benefit. "If you then, though you are evil, know how to give good gifts to your children, how much more will your Father in heaven give the Holy Spirit to those who ask him!" (Luke 11:13; see also Matthew 7:11)

The Holy Spirit continues to be active in the New Testament influencing the development and understanding of the Church, which at the time was being created and matured. Paul indicates the Church is then no longer a slave to sin but is adopted as children of God and heirs of the promise. (See Romans 8:14-17). Further,

> You, however, are not in the realm of the flesh but are in the realm of the Spirit, if indeed the Spirit of God lives in you. And if anyone does not have the Spirit of Christ, they do not belong to Christ. But if Christ is in you, then even though your body is subject to death because of sin, the Spirit gives life because of righteousness. And if the Spirit of him who raised Jesus from the dead is living in you, he who raised Christ from the dead will also give life to your mortal bodies because of his Spirit who lives in you. (Romans 8:9-11)

The Holy Spirit came to do what the law was powerless to do; to assist people to live in the realm of the Spirit, after accepting Jesus Christ as Saviour and Lord.

In Acts 2 we learn that the Holy Spirit, whose work is being now revealed in the New Testament, came with a different purpose than just to influence the truth of the prophets' proclamations and the development of the Bible. The development of the New Testament indicates that a main purpose of the Holy Spirit was to then instigate the creation of the Church and its maturing. He was to be inserted into the Church itself, through the baptism of the believer in the Holy Spirit, Himself. The Holy Spirit, at Pentecost, enabled the Church to be the Church.

> When the day of Pentecost came, they were all together in one place. Suddenly a sound like the blowing of a violent wind came from heaven and filled the whole house where they were sitting. They saw what seemed to be tongues of fire that separated and came to rest on each of them. All of them were filled with the Holy Spirit and began to speak in other tongues as the Spirit enabled them. (Acts 2:1-4)

The same Holy Spirit who hovered over the creation of the universe, came, empowered and filled the fledgling Church. He gave instruction to the Church through its writers, inspired by Himself. "In my former book, Theophilus, I wrote about all that Jesus began to do and to teach until the day he was taken up to heaven, after giving instructions through the Holy Spirit to the apostles he had chosen" (Acts 1:1-2). Here Dr. Luke referred to his own writing in the Gospel of Luke.

The Holy Spirit continues to be active in the creation and on-going growth of the Church as He was in the creation of the Old Testament, its prophecies and the results that always truly came to pass in the New Testament writings. He continues to work after Jesus left the earth having been resurrected to life eternal. These ongoing activities of the Holy Spirit were earlier suggested by Jesus Himself, in John's Gospel, to continue on after Jesus' death and resurrection. (See John 14:16-25). "But the Advocate, the Holy Spirit, whom the Father will send in my name, will teach you all things and will remind you of everything I have said to you" (John 14:26).

The current cultures of today do not know the Holy Spirit and His ongoing work, through the preached Word and in the living Church. Today's world is made up of various cultures, of all peoples on earth no matter the human or anthropological descriptions of differences: color, gender, size and intelligence potential. Scripture indicates that this world is wrong about its understanding of and respect for the doctrine of sin. Job's friend heard Job say, "I am pure, I have done no wrong; I am clean and free from sin" (Job 33:9). This is a worldly view. Paul summarized several Old Testament texts, "As it is written: 'There is no one righteous, not even one; there is no one who understands; there is no one who seeks God. All have turned away, they have together become worthless; there is no one who does good, not even one'" (Romans 3:10-12). Then Paul wrote to the Romans, "For all have sinned and fall short of the glory of God (Romans 3:23); and, "For the wages of sin is death, but the gift of God is eternal life in Christ Jesus our LORD" (Romans 6:23). (Also see Appendix 1). Meanwhile Believers, who are within all cultures and nations in the world are the Church, today.

The gospel of John also noted Jesus' words regarding the future influence of the Holy Spirit in the world. (See John 15:26-16:15). Jesus leaving the world at His resurrection meant the Holy Spirit would come amongst the church.

The Holy Spirit continues to work within the Church to tell the world Who God is. Just as Jesus was leaving the earth after His resurrection, He gave the Authority to establish and build the one true Church which was given to Him by the Holy Spirit. (See Matthew 28:18-20). This same Holy Spirit resides in the Church and continues to work after Jesus Christ returned to heaven.

You, however, are not in the realm of the flesh but are in the realm of the Spirit, if indeed the Spirit of God lives in you. And if anyone does not have the Spirit of Christ, they do not belong to Christ. But if Christ is in you, then even though your body is subject to death because of sin, the Spirit gives life because of righteousness. And if the Spirit of him who raised Jesus from the dead is living in you, he who raised Christ from the dead will also give life to your mortal bodies because of his Spirit who lives in you. (Romans 8:9-11)

The Holy Spirit continues to work amongst the Church to speak on the behalf of believers everywhere. Jesus reminded his followers,

You must be on your guard. You will be handed over to the local councils and flogged in the synagogues. On account of me you will stand before governors and kings as witnesses to them. And the gospel must first be preached to all nations. Whenever you are arrested and brought to trial, do not worry beforehand about what to say. Just say whatever is given you at the time, for it is not you speaking, but the Holy Spirit. (Mark 13:9-11; see also Luke 12:12; John 14:26)

The original biblical challenge, which was what was given to Israel by the Father because Abram heard the Lord (See Genesis 12:1-4) and recorded in the Old Testament, continues to be the challenge presented to the Church, following Christ's resurrection. Currently, within the Church, the Holy Spirit intercedes for each of us as we pray, preach, testify to our faith and seek all truth. Again, John 16:13, "But when he, the Spirit of truth, comes, he will guide you into all the truth. He will not speak on his own; he will speak only what he hears, and he will tell you what is yet to come." And He continues to empower the Church, "But you will receive power when the Holy Spirit comes on you; and you will be my witnesses in Jerusalem, and in all Judea and Samaria, and to the ends of the earth" (Acts 1:8).

Most importantly the Holy Spirit not only used the writings of the prophets in predicting the birth, life, death and resurrection of the Messiah which came to pass, the Holy Spirit also built within the scriptures a planned completion of the salvation of all peoples through the return of Jesus, a Second Coming, sometime in the future and a permanent restoration of saved humanity to eternal life.

Reference to Jesus' return is throughout this same Scripture. In Mark's Gospel, chapter 13, Jesus' teaching reflects on what has become known as the 'End Times'. In Mark 13:31-2 He notes first an important reference to the Bible, then refers to the end which is yet to come, "Heaven and earth will pass away, but my words will never pass away. But about that day or hour no one knows, not even the angels in heaven, nor the Son, but only the Father." In Revelation 1:7 the writer, under the influence of the same Holy Spirit, writes, "Look, he is coming with the clouds," and, "every eye will see him, even those who pierced him"; and, "all peoples on earth will mourn because of him. So, shall it be! Amen." His quote at the end comes from an Old Testament prophet. Zechariah wrote, "And I will pour out on the house of David and the inhabitants of Jerusalem a spirit of grace and supplication. They will look on me, the one they have pierced, and they will mourn for him as one mourns for an only child, and grieve bitterly for him as one grieves for a firstborn son" (Zechariah 12:10). The writer of Revelation is suggesting this is a reference to Jesus' return. Israel, with all peoples, will mourn as Jesus is recognized, in the end. This same writer notes, "Look, I am coming soon! My reward is with me, and I will give to each person according to what they have done. I am the Alpha and the Omega, the First and the Last, the Beginning and the End" (Revelation 22:12-13). The Holy Spirit in this last chapter in the Bible ties it all together, from beginning in Genesis to this end and Triumph.

This latter event has not happened yet, of course, but the assurance of such an event is secure based on the evidence in the Bible that the predicted coming of the Messiah, His life, death and resurrection has already occurred, as prophesied and recorded! Such is the hope of the Christian Church in our world today!

The key thought here is not so much who the Holy Spirit used to author the Biblical narrative, but that He did. I have recalled, over the many years of my pastoral ministry, my mother's comments to me when I was a high school student dealing with topics like the apparent contradiction between the accounts of Creation and high school science, at the time. She said, "It's not so important to believe God created the world in 7 literal 24 hour days but that one does not go so far as to say that God couldn't have created the world in 7 literal 24 hour days". There remains in me this firm belief that as scientific 'conclusions' change over time, my conviction is that the Holy Spirit remains the One responsible for what Bible was intended to be: "God's communication to humankind". One of my professors, who at the time had taught in seminary for many years, stated in a class that "when science and faith seem to contradict each other, I just wait". (Dr. Clyde Francisco).

In a response to the consideration of other gods, Isaiah speaks to Israel about God the Father,

> Listen to me, you descendants of Jacob,
>   all the remnant of the people of Israel,
> you whom I have upheld since your birth,
>   and have carried since you were born.
> Even to your old age and gray hairs
>   I am he, I am he who will sustain you.
> I have made you and I will carry you;
>   I will sustain you and I will rescue you.
>
> With whom will you compare me or count me equal?
>   To whom will you liken me that we may be compared?"

(Isaiah 46:3-5)

He states, "Who do you think God is?" And further,

> Remember this, keep it in mind,
>   take it to heart, you rebels.
> Remember the former things, those of long ago;
>   I am God, and there is no other;
>   I am God, and there is none like me.
> I make known the end from the beginning,

from ancient times, what is still to come.
I say, 'My purpose will stand,
   and I will do all that I please.' (Isaiah 46:8-10)

Through the prophet, under the influence of the Holy Spirit, the Father clarifies once again, to Israel, Who He is. And Jeremiah likewise, in responding to Israel's use of the neighbors' idols,

But the Lord is the true God;
   he is the living God, the eternal King.
When he is angry, the earth trembles;
   the nations cannot endure his wrath. (Jeremiah 10:10)

Students of scripture during the last several centuries have made contrasts between the writings of, for example, Peter and Paul. Such suggestions are a result, in part, of the biblical criticism of an earlier day that encouraged or created some problems with the text, for readers of the Bible, today. Finding conflicting ideas between two of the writers of the New Testament, for example, who were writing under the influence of the same Holy Spirit suggests that the Holy Spirit was therefore authoring contrasting and conflicting ideas or teaching, within the same scriptures. When challenged about His relationship with Satan by the religious leaders, Jesus commented about a kingdom divided, not being able to stand.

And the teachers of the law who came down from Jerusalem said, "He is possessed by Beelzebul! By the prince of demons he is driving out demons." So Jesus called them over to him and began to speak to them in parables: "How can Satan drive out Satan? If a kingdom is divided against itself, that kingdom cannot stand. If a house is divided against itself, that house cannot stand." (Mark 3:22-25)

If authors of the Biblical text wrote apparently contradictory messages within that same scripture that all of us have received, through and including prophecy, then the Kingdom of the Father will not stand, according to Jesus. So, it therefore follows according to Mark that if the Holy Spirit who used some of what Peter and Paul eventually stated and/or wrote includes conflicting verses or experiences, then it would seem, rather, that the material is not fully understood and needs more study.

Consider that a person, created in the image of the Father with adequate brain and thinking power is simply not able to piece an apparent confusion, at some given time. Since Timothy indicated "that all scripture is inspired" there seems to be no way to justify suggestions of conflicting themes. The conflict, which is often apparent at different times and regarding different subjects, is in one's understanding of what the writers seem to be communicating. The problem for me now and when I studied biblical criticism in seminary in the 1960's was that the matter of confusion is in one's own understanding of the texts, not confusion within the texts themselves. For us to presume that the work of the Holy Spirit in scripture can be completely figured out by finite minds, with created limitations in the first place, is humorous to say the least. Isaiah reminds us,

> Seek the Lord while he may be found;
>   call on him while he is near.
> Let the wicked forsake their ways
>   and the unrighteous their thoughts.
> Let them turn to the Lord, and he will have mercy on them,
>   and to our God, for he will freely pardon.

> "For my thoughts are not your thoughts,
>   neither are your ways my ways,"
>   declares the Lord.
> "As the heavens are higher than the earth,
>   **so are my ways higher than your ways**
>   and my thoughts than your thoughts". (Isaiah 55:6-9)

This same Bible, which we have been researching, indicates that the 'ways of the Father' are different than the 'ways of people'. The ways of people and their understanding has some limits …limits in our understanding of creation etc.

For example: A car is made with limits of speed. Because of demands in an economy, it needs to meet certain specifications and no further. So, with our own understanding of the world in which we live, our Father has placed 'limits' of some sort on our ability to 'see' or comprehend the world around us. "The fear of the LORD is the beginning of wisdom; all who follow his precepts have good understanding. To him belongs eternal praise" (Psalm 111:10). "Tell them this: 'These gods, who did not make the heavens and the earth, will perish from the earth and from under the heavens'. But God made the earth by his power; he founded the world by his wisdom and stretched out the heavens by his understanding" (Jeremiah 10:11-12). God made the heavens. "If any of you lacks wisdom, you should ask God, who gives generously to all without finding fault, and it will be given to you. But when you ask, you must believe and not doubt, because the one who doubts is like a wave of the sea, blown and tossed by the wind. That person should not expect to receive anything from the Lord" (James 1:5-7). Anyone who lacks wisdom?

> For the message of the cross is foolishness to those who are perishing, but to us who are being saved it is the power of God. For it is written: "I will destroy the wisdom of the wise; the intelligence of the intelligent I will frustrate." Where is the wise person? Where is the teacher of the law? Where is the philosopher of this age? Has not God made foolish the wisdom of the world? For since in the wisdom of God the world through its wisdom did not know him, God was pleased through the foolishness of what was preached to save those who believe. Jews demand signs and Greeks look for wisdom, but we preach Christ crucified: a stumbling block to Jews and foolishness to Gentiles, but to those whom God has called, both Jews and Greeks, Christ the power of God and the wisdom of God. For the foolishness of God is wiser than human wisdom, and the weakness of God is stronger than human strength. (1 Cor 1:18-25; see also Isaiah 29:14)

The proof, then, of the Holy Spirit's role in bringing us the Bible is that of its **truth.** Hence the Bible is currently able to measure all other religions' spiritual writings and oral tradition produced by all peoples throughout human history. It is a plumb line, exacting in its critique. The prophet, together with the Holy Spirit and the confirmation of events, predicted and actuated over centuries, even to the present, confirm its authenticity.

Endnotes

1. James Watson & Francis Crick, *Brilliant Research and Twisted Logic,* https://breakpoint.org/brilliant-research-twisted-logic/

Chapter 9

A BELIEVERS' RESPONSE: Kindness

As you have followed along with me throughout this book what response, among many options, might you give to the material that you have read and considered? Response to truth varies with people who read about it. Your response is critical as you reflect on the significance of the Bible as it has been brought to you, over many millennia. I am particularly interested in making the suggestion that your response be specific and determined. Responses to truth must bring community together, not create or influence division. If you are a believer through an understanding of the way the Bible describes it (see Appendix A and B) a response is needed and is critical. In the end our response can make a difference in our world; a difference in how you and I communicate 'Who God is' to those around us.

Consider then, that material presented in this book is based on the Truth of the Word of God. It states that this Scripture is for all people. It is the only oral and written sacred text that measures all other oral and written texts, created by sincere human intent throughout all of time. The Bible is the plumb line that measures truth; truth about the world, truth about God the Father, Son and Holy Spirit. It is God's Word given to us all, on all parts of the globe, involving all languages, all colors and all creeds, for all of time. To the church at Galatia Paul wrote, "There is neither Jew nor Gentile, neither slave nor free, nor is there male and female, for you are all one in Christ Jesus" (Galatians 3:28). So there is no "Them-Us" within the Church.

The Bible has been brought to all peoples through the intentional work of the Holy Spirit using human thoughts, experiences, inspiration and direction. Humans moved by the Holy Spirit heard and wrote the truth, initiated by the Father, to bring humankind back to a relationship with the one true God. According to this same scripture humanity is lost. Through the work of the Cross, humanity can and is being redeemed and restored to a right relationship with the Father. And contained within your Bible is the only one true message to the world about Who God is and the eventual conclusion of this human experiment, on earth. (See Appendix A)

We have been reminded within this book that the Bible has been criticized over the centuries partly because of its importance, which in the end is a spiritual matter. Having the Bible being looked at with critical eyes and thought is not necessarily wrong, but has occasionally proven to undermine the Bible's influence in various historical periods. We have briefly examined what has become known as Biblical criticism. It, as well, has tended to propagate the idea of dividing up the Bible into parts that are influenced by the Holy Spirit and parts that are not so influenced, according to certain criteria.

We have also come to discover afresh several key factors in the development of the Bible, over many centuries. The Holy Spirit has been and continues to be active in the influence of the Bible from the very beginning of its creation. He used ordinary people to communicate the Truths of God's Word, to follow His commands and to let the world around know Who He is. He used prophets, who had a specific calling and role, to communicate the Truth of the Father's creation of the world, the love of the Father for us all and for the eventual culmination of this experiment of Creation. We learned that the prophet was eventually always right, or he or she was not a true prophet. We have discovered afresh that the proof of the validity of the Bible is to be used as a plumb line against which to measure all other religious writing and oral traditions, over all time.

Being convinced of this Truth to the best of our understanding, what are believers the world over to do with such confidence in Biblical truth? Our response is critical in our world, in whatever culture we are living today. In whatever political or religious climate you and I are facing we, as believers, have a task. It is the same task given to Israel in the Old Testament and given to the Church in the New Testament. It is to tell the world around us Who God is. We believers are the Church. This task is given to the Church by the same Holy Spirit that instigated communication with Abraham, the early prophets and writers of Scripture. It is that Holy Spirit that continues to communicate to believers the world over, through regeneration and faith in Jesus Christ as Lord and Saviour of humankind. The writer of Ecclesiastes noted, "I have seen the burden God has laid on the human race. He has made everything beautiful in its time. He has also set eternity in the human heart, yet no one can fathom what God has done from beginning to end" (Ecclesiastes 3:10-11). Paul wrote to the Corinthians indicating that this experience of communicating to the world 'Who God is' must be a pleasant event rather than an unpleasant one. He put it this way: 'a pleasing aroma'. Note,

> But thanks be to God, who always leads us as captives in Christ's triumphal procession and uses us to spread the aroma of the knowledge of him everywhere. For we are to God the pleasing aroma of Christ among those who are being saved and those who are perishing. To the one we are an aroma that brings death; to the other, an aroma that brings life. And who is equal to such a task? Unlike so many, we do not peddle the word of God for profit. On the contrary, in Christ we speak before God with sincerity, as those sent from God. (2 Corinthians 2:14-17)

With this challenge and knowledge, while continuing to be involved in this task at whatever level, a believer's critical and **main response** is, I believe, to be one of **KINDNESS**. Being convinced of the truth of the Bible is a heady challenge. Arrogance is certainly one possible response a woman or man could have and that too has been modeled, unfortunately, throughout church history, along with other equally disarming emotions and actions. But kindness is the response that must be addressed in this final chapter. In fact, there is no more truthful and wholesome response to learning the truth of the Bible, than for believers to be kind, in every circumstance. "Those who are kind benefit themselves, but the cruel bring ruin on themselves" (Proverbs 11:17). Sometimes being kind is more important than being right. (Attributed to F. Scott Fitzgerald)

I realize kindness is a difficult response to pull off, in a moment of reaction, in so many cases. In my world, it is the response in traffic. People seem so rude! In my world, it involves dealing with family matters; gotta love them. In my world, it involves deep philosophical discussions and even political ones. What about in your world? Maybe it relates to waiting for water. Maybe it involves being in prison; or being in prison for wrong reasons. It could involve being kind when feeling alone. We live in a world where others come across as more important than us, often at their instigation. The truth of the claims of the Bible in any society can be very threatening. Varied responses to what you and I now know, given the nature of human power and its misuse, will continue to be threatening to believers anywhere in the world today by those outside of the faith; those who are not believers. There will also, of course, be many who will simply not care what the Bible is or how it might contribute to the world's needs.

But the "Them-Us" mentality, tribalism as I have called it, potentially excludes us all, from acting **kindly**. This experience of individual and corporate conflict exists in tribal communities; it is in first world communities as well, of course. When one has become convinced of the Authority of the Bible, created for ALL people, given in the context of an eternal Love by the Father, one must consider the significant idea that what is stated in our Bible, albeit in the original languages, is Truth for all time, for all people. "When we are slandered, we answer kindly" (1Corinthians 4:13a).

A BELIEVERS' RESPONSE: KINDNESS

The apostle Paul wrote to the believers in Colossae, "Therefore, as God's chosen people, holy and dearly loved, clothe yourselves with compassion, kindness, humility, gentleness and patience" (Colossians 3:12). John Wesley, an 18th century Anglican minister wrote,

> Condemn no man for not thinking as you think. Let everyone enjoy the full and free liberty of thinking for himself. Let every man use his own judgment, since every man must give an account of himself to God. Abhor every approach, in any kind or degree, to the spirit of persecution, if you cannot reason nor persuade a man into the truth, never attempt to force a man into it. If love will not compel him to come, leave him to God, the judge of all.

And here's an illustration in kindness: A child who has two apples and bites both… before giving one to Mom and saying "this one is the sweetest".

As I reflected on this material, I was reminded of some music that has become important to me, over the years. The first piece to which I refer below came to my awareness in the 1990's during the height of the Promise Keepers' movement.[1] Maranatha Music released "Live A Legacy" in 1998. Under the title, which I assume was prompted somewhat by this text from Esther 4:14, "For if you remain silent at this time, relief and deliverance for the Jews will arise from another place, but you and your father's family will perish. And who knows but that you have come to your royal position for such a time as this?", the song was written "For such a time as this". I have been challenged to write this book since 2009, several years after I retired from full time pastoral ministry. The challenge stayed with me over the years and in 2019, my wife and I decided I would put the effort and time into this work. These following words therefore, have been an influence on me keeping at this writing.

"We've been summoned here by God for such a time as this. We will not be silent, we will not hold back, By His grace we will rise up, for such a time as this. To make a difference in our generation, to advance His Kingdom on every side." I write for just such a time, in my world.

A second piece of music that has been an encouragement for me to continue over these years came from Stan Rogers' lyrics of *The Field Behind the Plow* which was sung by Chor Leoni, a Vancouver, BC, men's choir. The important words, for me, are found in verse four,

> Well in an hour, maybe more, you'll be wet clear through
> The air is cooler now, pull your hat brim further down
> And watch the field behind the plow turn to straight dark rows
> Put another seasons promise in the ground.

Investing time and work into a book is just that: work. It is so much like a farmer (the definition of my name, George, is 'a farmer') who faithfully continues in all weather to get the job done, knowing that work pays off, people benefit, family is blessed. This work is for the Kingdom, our family of believers who need encouragement in these days, in the culture in which you live, work and raise a family or are in a family.

The place and importance of kindness has already been modeled to us by the Father and in the Old Testament witness to the nature of God. In spite of the failure of Israel throughout the witness of the Old Testament to successfully tell the world Who God is, God indicated through the prophet, in Deuteronomy 4:31, "For the LORD your God is a merciful God; he will not abandon or destroy you or forget the covenant with your ancestors, which he confirmed to them by oath". Following this promise to Israel the writer, under the inspiration of the Holy Spirit said though Moses,

> Ask now about the former days, long before your time, from the day God created human beings on the earth; ask from one end of the heavens to the other. Has anything so great as this ever happened, or has anything like it ever been heard of? Has any other people heard the voice of God speaking out of fire, as you

have, and lived? Has any god ever tried to take for himself one nation out of another nation, by testings, by signs and wonders, by war, by a mighty hand and an outstretched arm, or by great and awesome deeds, like all the things the LORD your God did for you in Egypt before your very eyes? You were shown these things so that you might know that the LORD is God; besides him there is no other. From heaven he made you hear his voice to discipline you. On earth he showed you his great fire, and you heard his words from out of the fire. Because he loved your ancestors and chose their descendants after them, he brought you out of Egypt by his Presence and his great strength, to drive out before you nations greater and stronger than you and to bring you into their land to give it to you for your inheritance, as it is today. Acknowledge and take to heart this day that the LORD is God in heaven above and on the earth below. There is no other. Keep his decrees and commands, which I am giving you today, so that it may go well with you and your children after you and that you may live long in the land the LORD your God gives you for all time. (Deuteronomy 4:32-40)

In this promise we recognize the ongoing kindness and love of the Father for Israel; the promise of ongoing care. We are here reminded of the creation of the world, through the Will of the Father. We are reminded that no other nation has heard His voice, no other god has had the ability or success to do for any other people what God has done for Israel. Verse 35 indicates that Israel was shown these things so that "you might know that the Lord is God; besides him there is no other".

Further in Jeremiah, "The LORD appeared to us in the past, saying: 'I have loved you with an everlasting love; I have drawn you with unfailing kindness'" (Jeremiah 31:3), and, "but let the one who boasts boast about this: that they have the understanding to know me, that I am the LORD, who exercises kindness, justice and righteousness on earth, for in these I delight," declares the LORD" (Jeremiah 9:24), or, "I will tell of the kindnesses of the LORD, the deeds for which he is to be praised, according to all the LORD has done for us - yes, the many good things he has done for Israel, according to his compassion and many kindnesses" (Isaiah 63:7), and, "'In a surge of anger I hid my face from you for a moment, but with everlasting kindness I will have compassion on you,' says the LORD your Redeemer" (Isaiah 54:8).

As the nation of Israel continued over the centuries to be less and less in touch with their God, He continued to intervene with kindness and one example is in Ezra, "Though we are slaves, our God has not forsaken us in our bondage. He has shown us kindness in the sight of the kings of Persia: He has granted us new life to rebuild the house of our God and repair its ruins, and he has given us a wall of protection in Judah and Jerusalem" (Ezra 9:9). Regarding the coming ages, as the Church took over this same task to inform all peoples, Paul told the Ephesians, "In order that in the coming ages he might show the incomparable riches of his grace, expressed in his kindness to us in Christ Jesus" (Ephesians 2:7).

Kindness is the order of the day for believers as well. Kindness has been modeled by the early church. Dr. Luke informed the early church of God's ongoing kindness and stated, "Yet he has not left himself without testimony: He has shown kindness by giving you rain from heaven and crops in their seasons; he provides you with plenty of food and fills your hearts with joy" (Acts 14:17). It is also nevertheless a conditional kindness. "Consider therefore the kindness and sternness of God: sternness to those who fell, but kindness to you, provided that you continue in his kindness. Otherwise, you also will be cut off" (Romans 11:22).

Kindness has a significant goal. Paul wrote to the Romans indicating that we are not the ones to judge others, just be kind. Judgment is left to Him, the Father.

> Now we know that God's judgment against those who do such things is based on truth. So when you, a mere human being, pass judgment on them and yet do the same things, do you think you will escape God's judgment? Or do you show contempt for the riches of his kindness, forbearance and patience, not realiz-

ing that God's kindness is intended to lead you to repentance?" (Romans 2:2-4)

Our kindness changes attitudes, even ours.

Further, the early church was told to continue to be kind, amongst other attributes by the apostle Paul, "But the fruit of the Spirit is love, joy, peace, forbearance, kindness, goodness, faithfulness" (Galatians 5:22), and, "in purity, understanding, patience and kindness; in the Holy Spirit and in sincere love" (2 Corinthians 6:6).

Kindness is modeled to us by writers of the New Testament as the Church began to grow in the first century, after Christ's birth, death and resurrection. "The islanders showed us unusual kindness. They built a fire and welcomed us all because it was raining and cold" (Acts 28:2). "The next day we landed at Sidon; and Julius, in kindness to Paul, allowed him to go to his friends so they might provide for his needs" (Acts 27:3).

Or,

The next day the rulers, the elders and the teachers of the law met in Jerusalem. Annas the high priest was there, and so were Caiaphas, John, Alexander and others of the high priest's family. They had Peter and John brought before them and began to question them: "By what power or what name did you do this?" Then Peter, filled with the Holy Spirit, said to them: "Rulers and elders of the people! If we are being called to account today for an act of kindness shown to a man who was lame and are being asked how he was healed, then know this, you and all the people of Israel: It is by the name of Jesus Christ of Nazareth, whom you crucified but whom God raised from the dead, that this man stands before you healed. Jesus is '"the stone you builders rejected, which has become the cornerstone.' Salvation is found in no one else, for there is no other name under heaven given to mankind by which we must be saved." (Acts 4:5-12)

Arrogance in response to our understanding of God's plan of salvation, which came to us from someone else's kindness, will never win the day. It will never foster community. It will never communicate to our world Who God is. "A gentle answer turns away wrath, but a harsh word stirs up anger" (Proverbs 15:1).

The model of action to be continually given by each believer, as demonstrated in the Bible, is that of kindness. It is demonstrated hundreds of times in other passages of scripture. The Church must act in our world with an attitude and example of kindness in the midst of this acquired knowledge of what the Bible is and how it came to ALL people: the knowledge of the purpose of the Bible and the importance of its dissemination world-wide. I continue to marvel at the actions of Believers around the world, those about whom I have read or met, who have placed their lives in jeopardy to get the Word out, to distribute Bibles. In this very year, through an unplanned incident with which I was involved, I met a young man who for many years travelled the US and Mexico distributing Bibles, on his 'own dime'.

As I am at my desk, completing this last chapter of *By What Authority*, I and my community have been living in the context of what will be known forever, as COVID 19. All around us, in our world, sickness and death have reigned in country after country. Our local medical leaders have sought, over these months, to express a 'model' of behavior that each person in our community might seriously consider demonstrating. It is one of **KINDNESS**. This recommended behavior has come to influence how we consider physical distancing. It has influenced how my community has dealt with the challenge to wear a mask, when in public, to 'protect others near us'. It is in this context, today and each day, that individuals make choices. Kindness is a choice when considering any social issue. It will always be a choice. It may often be a split-second choice, even a difficult one, but the right choice in the end.

Oh, and after you have read this book please consider passing it on to someone you care about.

Endnotes

1	https://promisekeepers.org/

BY WHAT AUTHORITY

Appendix A

THE SALVATION PLAN

Browsing? Curious? I appreciate you have picked this book up. You may be in some difficulty just now.

Maybe you are not at peace.

Maybe you have hurt someone and not sought forgiveness.

Or you are in prison.

Maybe you are in prison and are looking at a lot of time, yet, there.

Maybe you have become very angry.

Or you are hooked on drugs.

Or you have left a spouse and/or some of your family and are 'absent'.

Maybe you are homeless and do not have any plan.

Or you have just found this book and are searching for some meaning to a life you have lived and in which you have not found much meaningfulness, at all. There is **HOPE** in this life.

Or while reading this book, you have come to understand or are coming to understand that the Word of God the Father, is for all people. He used willing people to communicate to the world, **Who He Is.** Believing that there is a God, believing that Jesus is the Son of

God and believing that we are all sinners, from our earliest years, we can then consider the plan of salvation which is briefly outlined below. It is a plan that is contained within the pages of the Bible, created on purpose by the Holy Spirit, for each of us to come to understand and then to do something about what we have learned. We must personally make a decision. For your interest and consideration, may the following be a light in your search for peace. Someone first explained this plan of salvation to me when I was around six years old. I did not get it all then, but began the journey with the Father at that time. I accepted Jesus as my Lord and Saviour, by hearing and then being led in a brief prayer. Over the years I have learned more, trusted more and still have a lot to learn. Consider the following for yourself. Start with praying, briefly, for some faith.

First, you must **agree** with God, that all are sinners. Paul writes to the Romans in summary,

> What shall we conclude then? Do we have any advantage? Not at all! For we have already made the charge that Jews and Gentiles alike are all under the power of sin. As it is written: "There is no one righteous, not even one; there is no one who understands; there is no one who seeks God. All have turned away, they have together become worthless; there is no one who does good, not even one" (Romans 3:9-12).

If we are to base our relationship with the Father on what we have done in this life, we are mistaken whoever we are, whatever faith we may have, in whatever religion we may have been raised or educated. "**For the wages of sin is death**, but the gift of God is eternal life in Christ Jesus our Lord" (Romans 6:23). The death referred to here is eternal death, separation from the Father for eternity. This means all of us. "For all have sinned and fall short of the glory of God" (Romans 3:23). Do you agree you are a sinner in the eyes of the Father?

APPENDIX A

Then **Second**, you need to **believe** with our whole heart and mind that Jesus died for your sins, to take away the penalty of all your sin, everything even if you can't remember all of it. He is God: "The Son is the image of the invisible God, the firstborn over all creation" (Colossians 1:15). The Gospel includes the simple fact that Jesus, God's one and only Son, came to this earth to pay for the penalty of the sins of all people, once for all, by dying on a cross, for humanity, for you.

> For God so loved the world that he gave his one and only Son, that whoever believes in him shall not perish but have eternal life. For God did not send his Son into the world to condemn the world, but to save the world through him. Whoever believes in him is not condemned, but whoever does not believe stands condemned already because they have not believed in the name of God's one and only Son. (John 3:16-18)

You may feel you are being condemned for your lifestyle and actions of sinfulness that you have done and now acknowledge. The Bible has clearly shown that that feeling of condemnation is as a result of sin in your life; **guilt** is another word for it. The prophet wrote that this is the case for all people, "We all, like sheep, have gone astray, each of us has turned to our own way; and the LORD has laid on him the iniquity of us all" (Isaiah 53:6). And Paul wrote to the Romans: But God demonstrates his own love for us in this, "While we were still sinners, Christ died for us" (Romans 5:8), and, "Yet to all who did receive him, to those who believed in his name, he gave the right to become children of God" (John 1:12). This worldwide family including all Believers, who have a faith in Christ, can include you.

The above text in John indicates that that condemnation does not need to remain. "How much more, then, will the blood of Christ, who through the eternal Spirit offered himself unblemished to God, cleanse our consciences from acts that lead to death, so that we may serve the living God!" (Hebrews 9:14). Simply believe and the penalty and guilt of sin leaves you, for ever.

And then **Third**, you must **confess** your sin to the Father, agreeing that you cannot come to Him on your own merit; your own good works. "If you declare with your mouth, "Jesus is Lord," and believe in your heart that God raised him from the dead, you will be saved" (Romans 10:9). There needs to be a personal acknowledgement of what you have now come to believe. You must take some action. It is called confession, in Jesus' name, to the Father. This confession can be done in private; with a simple prayer of repentance in the Name of Jesus. It can be done with the assistance and encouragement of a pastor or Christian friend, believing loved one or parent. (see a sample prayer, below).

Finally, **Four, do something** with this new experience of faith in Jesus Christ. "For it is by grace you have been saved, through faith- and this is not from yourselves, it is the gift of God- not by works, so that no one can boast. For we are God's handiwork, created in Christ Jesus to do good works, which God prepared in advance for us to do" (Ephesians 2:8-10). From now on, you can begin to tell the world around you, Who God Is. This is a challenge for all of us, throughout all human history. To the Corinthians, Paul wrote,

> What, after all, is Apollos? And what is Paul? Only servants, through whom you came to believe-as the LORD has assigned to each his task. I planted the seed, Apollos watered it, but God has been making it grow. So neither the one who plants nor the one who waters is anything, but only God, who makes things grow. The one who plants and the one who waters have one purpose, and they will each be rewarded according to their own labor. For we are co-workers in God's service; you are God's field, God's building. (1 Corinthians 3:5-9)

Paul encouraged the Corinthians to carry on the work of telling the world Who God is; each according to their gifts and experience.

If you today, can see the need for Jesus in your life from now on, can see the need of forgiveness, can see the need for the power of the Holy Spirit to live within you, in order to live the mandate of the Christian life, take the step of accepting Jesus Christ as your Savior and Lord. Then we can together say with Paul who wrote to the Romans,

> For I am not ashamed of the gospel, because it is the power of God that brings salvation to everyone who believes: first to the Jew, then to the Gentile. For in the gospel the righteousness of God is revealed-a righteousness that is by faith from first to last, just as it is written: "The righteous will live by faith." (Romans 1:16-17)

A SIMPLE PRAYER FOR YOU:

Dear Father, I confess that I have sinned. I have done what is displeasing to you and have hurt others, including myself, by my acts of sin. I believe Jesus is your Son and died on the Cross to pay the penalty for the sin of all people, including me. In the Name of Jesus, Your Son, please accept my prayer of confession for all my sin and forgive me, through Jesus' work of death on the Cross. I believe He rose again and is retuning someday. I turn from my sins and believe You have heard my prayer. Thank You, Father, for forgiving me today. Amen.

BY WHAT AUTHORITY

Appendix B

ASSURANCE OF FAITH IN CHRIST

One of the most satisfying experiences I have had over the many years of pastoral ministry is to engage with a person who is a believer, who has professed faith in Jesus Christ as Lord and Saviour but who is not sure of their salvation. This lack of assurance can occur in a believer's life for many reasons, long after they have become a believer. They have known and experienced, as Luke wrote in Acts 2:21, where Peter is quoting from Joel 2:32, "And everyone who calls on the name of the Lord will be saved. They will have remembered the scripture: "Everyone who calls on the name of the Lord will be saved" (Romans 10:13). They were able to recall, maybe, that this text applied to them at one time. They believed, at one time, Jesus's words in John 14:6, "Jesus answered, 'I am the way and the truth and the life. No one comes to the Father except through me."

But at the time of our meeting, they were no longer sure of their faith and are inquiring, as to that assurance. Whatever the context of their life that had caused the doubt, they have come to a place where they are willing to inquire about this subject. Often it was as result of a sermon or some discussion with a friend or family member. At this point one can begin thinking of the implications of Jesus' challenge in Revelation.

Here I am! I stand at the door and knock. If anyone hears my voice and opens the door, I will come in and eat with that person, and they with me. To the one who is victorious, I will give the right to sit with me on my throne, just as I was victorious and sat down with my Father on his throne. Whoever has ears, let them hear what the Spirit says to the churches. (Revelation 3:20-22)

Through the writing of John, the Holy Spirit gives some assurance of one's faith in the Person of Jesus Christ. It is a very personal and intimate encounter. It is at a door, the door of your own heart. It involves hearing a voice and a promise.

Then one might look at 1 John 5:6-12,

This is the one who came by water and blood—Jesus Christ. He did not come by water only, but by water and blood. And it is the Spirit who testifies, because the Spirit is the truth. **For there are three that testify: The Spirit, the water and the blood; and the three are in agreement.** We accept human testimony, but God's testimony is greater because it is the testimony of God, which he has given about his Son. Whoever believes in the Son of God accepts this testimony. Whoever does not believe God has made him out to be a liar, because they have not believed the testimony God has given about his Son. And this is the testimony: God has given us eternal life, and this life is in his Son. Whoever has the Son has life; whoever does not have the Son of God does not have life.

John makes reference to the Holy Spirit, still very active in the life of the Church. One believes and accepts this testimony. Having already done that one reads that John then indicated, in the context of explaining the work of faith in Jesus Christ through the Holy Spirit, that **if you have the Son**, you have life (eternal life) and i**f you do not have the Son**, you do not have eternal life. Pretty clear. This is the Word of God, to you.

Next consider 1 John 5:13-15, "I write these things to you who believe in the name of the Son of God so that you may know that you have eternal life. This is the confidence we have in approaching

God: that if we ask anything according to his will, he hears us. And if we know that he hears us—whatever we ask—we know that we have what we asked of him". Here John continued to nail down assurance. To you who believe in the name of the Son of God, you can KNOW you have eternal life. To know, using the Greek word for know in this context, is to know by experience. You can know for certain, by your experience of the Father: not wonder, not hope, not speculate, not question. This certainty of assurance comes from God's Word, to you. One can know they have what was promised, no matter how they might be feeling, at times. We know that we have what we asked of Him.

To "you who believe" John wrote. I have referred to believers throughout this book. I have defined them or us, from the Bible. For us there has been an event in our lives, at some point, where we have professed faith in Jesus Christ as Lord and Saviour and John is writing to us, to YOU.

To the Corinthians, Paul wrote,

> So from now on we regard no one from a worldly point of view. Though we once regarded Christ in this way, we do so no longer. Therefore, if anyone is in Christ, the new creation has come: the old has gone, the new is here! All this is from God, who reconciled us to himself through Christ and gave us the ministry of reconciliation: that God was reconciling the world to himself in Christ, not counting people's sins against them. And he has committed to us the message of reconciliation. We are therefore Christ's ambassadors, as though God were making his appeal through us. We implore you on Christ's behalf: Be reconciled to God. God made him who had no sin to be sin for us, so that in him we might become the righteousness of God. (2 Corinthians 5:16-21)

Our challenge then, is to tell the world around us, Who God is. This has always been the challenge to humanity. By the work of Christ on the Cross, the Church is empowered to do just that. Praise His Name!!

About the Author

Dr. George Edgar Sears

Born and raised in Edmonton, Alberta, Canada

Further education included a Bachelor of Arts degree, from the University of Alberta in 1967, a Master of Divinity degree from Southern Baptist Theological Seminary in 1971 and a Doctor of Ministry degree from Fuller Seminary in 1997.

George married Judith Russell in 1966. They have four married children and ten grandchildren. Dr. Sears was ordained to the Gospel Ministry by the American Baptist Convention in 1970.

George served as a Senior and/or Associate Pastor in Indiana, Manitoba, Alberta and British Columbia from 1969 to 2006, after which he and Judith retired from active pastoring. Since retirement George has served North American Baptists and Canadian Baptists as an Interim Pastor, Chair of Carey Theological College from 2011 to 2017 and as an Associate Chaplain at Vancouver International Airport, since 2007. *BY WHAT AUTHORITY* is Dr. Sears' first book. He was earlier published: Claussen, D. S., ed. Standing on The Promises. (Cleveland, Ohio, Pilgrim Press, 1999) *The Need to Develop Male Friendship*, chapter 6, p. 61-71.

Made in the USA
Columbia, SC
08 June 2023